# Immortal Sayings

From Indian Scriptures and Classics

Dr. B. R. Suhas

*Published by:*

F-2/16, Ansari road, Daryaganj, New Delhi-110002
☎ 23240026, 23240027 • *Fax:* 011-23240028
*Email:* info@vspublishers.com • *Website:* www.vspublishers.com

**Branch : Hyderabad**
5-1-707/1, Brij Bhawan (Beside Central Bank of India Lane)
Bank Street, Koti Hyderabad - 500 095
☎ 040-24737290
*E-mail:* vspublishershyd@gmail.com

**Distributors :**

- **Pustak Mahal®**, Delhi
  J-3/16, Daryaganj, New Delhi-110002
  ☎ 23276539, 23272783, 23272784 • *Fax:* 011-23260518
  *E-mail:* sales@pustakmahal.com • *Website:* www.pustakmahal.com
  Bengaluru: ☎ 080-22234025 • *Telefax:* 080-22240209
  Patna: ☎ 0612-3294193 • *Telefax:* 0612-2302719

- **PM Publications**
  - 10-B, Netaji Subhash Marg, Daryaganj, New Delhi-110002
    ☎ 23268292, 23268293, 23279900 • *Fax:* 011-23280567
    *E-mail:* pmpublications@gmail.com
  - 6686, Khari Baoli, Delhi-110006
    ☎ 23944314, 23911979

- **Unicorn Books**
  Mumbai :
  23-25, Zaoba Wadi, (Opp. VIP Showroom), Thakurdwar, Mumbai-400002
  ☎ 022-22010941 • *Telefax:* 022-22053387

© **Copyright:** V&S PUBLISHERS
ISBN 978-93-813845-5-8
**Edition : 2011**

---

The Copyright of this book, as well as all matter contained herein (including illustrations) rests with the Publishers. No person shall copy the name of the book, its title design, matter and illustrations in any form and in any language, totally or partially or in any distorted form. Anybody doing so shall face legal action and will be responsible for damages.

---

*Printed at :* Unique Colour Carton, Mayapuri

*Dedicated to my Father,
Er. B.G. Ramesh.
A great writer and an
inspiration for my writing.*

# Contents

*Preface* ............................................................................. 7
Invocation ....................................................................... 9
Appraisal of Good Words .......................................... 10
Appraisal of Poets and Poetry .................................. 13
Knowledge and Education ........................................ 15
Learning and Earning ................................................ 20
Useless Knowledge and Money ................................ 24
Money ........................................................................... 26
Miser .............................................................................. 29
Generosity and Charity .............................................. 30
Useless Charity ............................................................ 34
Rich and Poor .............................................................. 35
Arts ................................................................................ 39
Occupation ................................................................... 41
Endeavour .................................................................... 44
Enthusiasm ................................................................... 46
Laziness ........................................................................ 48
Action and Divinity ................................................... 52
Evils of Men and Women ......................................... 54
Merits and Demerits .................................................. 58
Heaven and Hell ......................................................... 60
Righteousness .............................................................. 63
Truth ............................................................................. 68
Non-violence ............................................................... 71
Service .......................................................................... 73
The Art of Speaking .................................................. 77

| | |
|---|---|
| The Intelligent and the Foolish | 82 |
| The Noble and the Wicked | 86 |
| Appraisal of Good Character | 94 |
| Modesty | 102 |
| Friendship | 104 |
| Relatives | 110 |
| Courage | 113 |
| Weakness | 117 |
| Self-respect | 118 |
| Mind | 120 |
| Happiness and Sorrow | 125 |
| Beauty | 131 |
| Desire | 133 |
| Anger | 136 |
| Contentment | 140 |
| Sacrifice | 142 |
| Fame | 143 |
| Foresight | 146 |
| Duty | 147 |
| Precious Jewels | 148 |
| Unity | 149 |
| Kings and Rulers | 150 |
| Master and Servant | 152 |
| Women | 153 |
| Teacher | 156 |
| Rarities | 158 |
| Always Wonderful | 160 |
| Elevation and Downfall | 161 |
| Death | 164 |
| Questions and Answers | 166 |
| Poison | 171 |
| Penance and Renouncement | 173 |
| God and the Soul | 176 |
| Devotion | 180 |
| Words of Wisdom | 183 |

# Preface

Sanskrit is one of the oldest languages of the world. Its rich heritage includes epics, religious and devotional scriptures, poetic works, dramas and other literary works. *Subhashitas* form a special feature of Sanskrit literature. *Subhashitas* are equivalent to proverbs and sayings found in other languages.

*Subhashitas* means "words of wisdom". *Subhashitas* are short verses or shlokas that convey thoughtful messages through elegant examples. As dry preaching does not hit the mark, *Subhashitas* preach through interesting examples in rhythmic poems. Such preaching is appreciated just as a sugar-coated bitter medicine is liked. The matter dealt in these *Subhashitas* is variegated and include such topics like appraisal of scholars, value of knowledge, money, good and bad, fools and the intelligent, moral lessons, courage, fear, self-respect, endeavour, enthusiasm, love, happiness and sorrow, laziness, truth, righteousness, friendship, sense control, God, devotion and many more. These *Subhashitas* consist of day-to-day experiences that everyone enjoys.

*Subhashitas* are present in large numbers throughout Sanskrit literary works. The Vedas, Upanishads, Mahabharata, Ramayana, Puranas, Panchatantra and the celebrated works of poets such as Kalidasa, Bhavabhuti, Kalhana, Bhartrihari etc are full of *Subhashitas*. Besides, there are individual works dedicated to a collection of *Subhashitas* like *Suktimuktavali, Subhashita Sudhanidhi, Subhashita Ratnabandagara, Samayochita Padyamalika, Narabharana* and many more. Scholars are collecting *Subhashitas* even today and many such collections like *Subhashita Manjari, Subhashita Ratnavali, Subhashita Samputa, Nitya Neeti* etc are in Kannada and English translations.

In this compilation of Sanskrit *Subhashitas*, I have made a sincere effort to convey the meaning of these *Subhashitas*. The translations are free and not literal. Short explanations have been added to each verse to appreciate the meaning and message of the *Subhashita*. I owe my thanks to many different sources I have referred to in preparing this compilation. I hope readers enjoy this book. I would like to receive feedback from readers via e-mail at: *brs_doc@yahoo.co.in*.

**—Dr B.R. Suhas**

# Invocation

1. दिक्कालाद्यनवच्छिन्नानन्तचिन्मात्रमूर्तये ।
   स्वानुभूत्येकमानाय नमः शान्ताय तेजसे ॥

*Obeisance unto the Lord, who is not bound by space and time, who is Infinite, whose form is knowledge personified, who is effulgent, peaceful, and who can be realised only by one's own experience.*

—Neeti Shataka - 1

It is always customary to start any work with a prayer to the Almighty Lord. This shloka appears in a composition called *Neetishataka*, a collection of 100 moral sayings composed by King Bhartrihari. In his prayer, he also describes the nature of God, saying that He is not bound by time and space. All of us have a limited body that is bound by space and time. The body is subject to time, and it has a beginning and an end. But God is Eternal; so also the Atma, but for the illusion. Thus, the body limits the Jiva. But God is Omnipresent. He is called Vishnu, which means all-pervading. Therefore, He is unlimited.

God is Omniscient. In the *Bhagavad Gita*, Lord Krishna says, "From all the Vedas, I am to be known." He is *Sat* (Truth), *Chit* (Knowledge) and *Ananda* (Bliss). He is self-effulgent, like the sun. He is peaceful and never gets afflicted by any situation. God can be realised only by one's own experience, through devotion and perseverance. It is not possible for anyone to 'show' Him. It is often said that the taste of sugar can be realised only by tasting it!

Obeisance to the Lord.

# Appraisal of Good Words

2. भाषासु मुख्या मधुरा दिव्या गीर्वाणभारती ।
तत्रापि काव्यं मधुरं तस्मादपि सुभाषितम् ॥

*Among all the languages, Sanskrit is the sweetest, most important and divine. And in this Sanskrit literature, poetry is sweeter, and among poetry, 'Subhashita' or 'good word' is the sweetest.*

—**Subhashita Ratna Bhandagara**

It is said that Sanskrit is the mother of all languages. It is the most ancient language. Historians say that the ancient Aryans transacted in this language, and tradition maintains that it is the language of Gods. The words *Geervani Bharati* in verse refers to this. The works composed in Sanskrit are all beautiful and many of the religious and literary works of India, like the Ramayana, Mahabharata, Puranas, Vedas, and Upanishads, are composed in Sanskrit. Many great poets like Kalidasa, Magha, Bhavabhuti, Dandi *et al.* wrote in Sanskrit and enriched our cultural heritage. These books bring out the scope of emotional joy.

Again, the verse form is an easier way of remembering the text and can also be sung in tunes. The poems contain words framed in a rhythmic manner that are pleasing to the ear. Among these poetic works, it is said that the *Subhashitas* are the sweetest, as they are very close to one's life, and have evolved from experiences of the great.

3. द्राक्षा म्लानमुखी जाता शर्करा चाश्मतां गता ।
सुभाषितरसस्याग्रे सुधा भीता दिवं गता ॥

*In the presence of nectarian Subhashita, grapes withered, sugar turned into stone, and even the nectar was afraid and ran up to heaven!*

—Subhashita Manjari

Here, the poet humorously glorifies the greatness of good works. All the sweet substances in the world fail to become great in the presence of *Subhashitas* or good sayings. The grapes that were very sweet to taste bent their heads down, and sugar turned into stone! And even nectar, which bestows immortality on one who drinks it, could not stand before such good sayings and fled to heaven!

The poet has made use of simile and metaphor to describe the greatness of divine thoughts.

4. पृथिव्यां त्रीणि रत्नानि जलमन्नं सुभाषितम् ।
मूढैः पाषाणखण्डेषु रत्नसंज्ञा विधीयते ॥

*There are three jewels on this earth, namely water, food, and good sayings. Only fools call stone pieces jewels.*

—Subhashita Manjari - 1.5

Here, the poet says that *Subhashitas*, noble thoughts, are like invaluable treasures, just as food and water are invaluable jewels, for without them no living being could exist on earth. These sayings protect a person when in difficulty, and if one lives according to such sayings of the great, his life blooms like a flower. Unfortunately, says the poet, fools are only interested in calling stone pieces jewels (wealth), which merely give temporary and external happiness.

5. संसारविषवृक्षस्य द्वे फले ह्यमृतोपमे ।
सुभाषितरसास्वादः सङ्गतिः सुजनैः सह ॥

*In the poisonous tree of life, there are two nectarean fruits. One of them is the tasty noble saying and the other is the company of noble people.*

—Subhashita Manjari - 1.8

Herein, the poet compares life to a poisonous tree. Everyone definitely experiences that life is miserable. One has to pass through a lot of hurdles to reach a goal and attain happiness, which is momentary. Though none of us like it, we are subject to failures, illness, old age, death, and many other difficulties. Thus, life is like a poisonous tree. But this thought should not make us quit. Even in such a poisonous tree there are two nectarean fruits – noble sayings and great people. Noble sayings can guide a person to lead a peaceful life. And if one befriends great people, who set an example for others by their hard work and achievements, one's life will be filled with harmony and happiness.

# Appraisal of Poets and Poetry

6. जयन्ति ते सुकृतिनो रससिद्धाः कवीश्वराः ।
नास्ति तेषां यशः काये जरामरणजं भयम् ॥

*The great poets, who have renowned themselves in poetry, never have to fear old age and death for they are immortal bodies of fame, and they are indeed victorious!*

— Neeti Shataka - 22

Poets are great people. They develop intimacy with nature and draw inspiration to live in harmony with the surroundings, which they communicate to others. These poets may grow old, or die, but it is their body that perishes, as they remain immortal through their memorable works. This brings to mind the story of Valmiki, the first poet of the world, who is hence called *Adikavi*. Lord Brahma granted him a boon that as long as the sun, the moon, lakes and mountains existed, so long would humans read his book, Ramayana. This statement holds true to this day, as the book has been translated into several languages, and has also been telecast in serial form.

Thus, poets are victorious.

7. अपारे काव्यसंसारे कविरेकः प्रजापतिः ।
यथास्मै रोचते विश्वं तथेदं परिवर्तते ॥

*In the vast world of literature, the poet alone is the creator. As he feels, so this world gets changed!*

— Dhvanya Loka - 3

In the world of literature, the poet is a creator in the sense that he can influence the direction of his created world. If he wishes rainfall, there is rainfall and if he wishes sunshine, there is sunshine. The poet creates different moods and converts his world into an attractive realm.

8. अवक्तापि स्वयं लोकः कामं काव्यपरीक्षकः ।
रसपाकानभिज्ञाऽपि भोक्ता वेत्ति न किं रसम् ॥

*One can appreciate the greatness of poetry, even if he is not a poet. It is just like a person who can enjoy the taste of cooked food, even if he does not know cooking.*

— Yashastilaka - 1.29

It is not necessary for a person to be a poet to appreciate the beauty of poetry. Although appreciating poetry is inherent in human nature, this sense of appreciation has to be developed. A person living in an environment of cruelty and wickedness may not be able to do so, for his nature would be different. On the other hand, a person who has trained his mind with noble thoughts would appreciate poetry even though he is not a poet. The poet compares this to a person who can appreciate the taste of good food, despite being unable to cook.

9. शास्त्रेषु दुर्ग्रहोप्यर्थः स्वदते कविसूक्तिषु ।
दृश्यं करगतं रत्नं दारुणं फणिमूर्धनि ॥

*The matter present in scriptures, though very difficult to understand, becomes easily understandable when presented in poetic verses. This is like a jewel that appears terrifying when it is on the head of a serpent.*

— Sabharanjana Shataka - 14

Great scriptures like the Vedas and the Upanishads teach man how he can lead a useful, productive, content and happy life. But for a common man, and even for the learned, their contents are difficult to understand. So, many poets, philosophers and saints appear on earth to teach us the same truth, which is compared to a jewel on a serpent's head that no one dares touch although everyone wishes to procure it.

# Knowledge and Education

10. विद्या नाम नरस्य रूपमधिकं प्रच्छन्नगुप्तं धनम् ।
    विद्या भोगकरी यशस्सुखकरी विद्या गुरूणां गुरुः ॥
    विद्या बन्धुजनो विदेशगमने विद्या परा देवता ।
    विद्या राजसु पूजिता न तु धनं विद्याविहीनः पशुः ॥

*Knowledge is a special beauty for man. It is a hidden treasure. It gives one happiness, enjoyment and fame. It is the teacher of great teachers. It is one's relative when he is in a foreign land. It is the God divine. It is knowledge that is worshipped by kings, and not money. One who is bereft of knowledge is a beast.*

—Neeti Shataka - 18

The poet Bhartrihari herein glorifies the various attributes of knowledge and learning. It imparts beauty to a man, he says. One can always compare an uneducated and an educated man and know the difference. The way of talking, behaviour and thoughts are all refined in an educated person. Reading and gaining knowledge is like a hidden treasure that helps one. If a person thus knows the language, ways and culture of different places, he can always communicate easily. Knowledge is Divine God, and it also helps one to know God.

The Lord has therefore said in the *Gita*, "There is nothing equal to knowledge." It is well known that in the past, kings would felicitate great poets and scholars, and not rich people. Thus, one who does not have knowledge is like a beast. Hence, everyone must read and learn more.

11. विद्या ददाति विनयं विनयाद्याति पात्रताम् ।
पात्रत्वाद्धनमाप्नोति धनाद्धर्मं ततः सुखम् ॥

*Education (knowledge) imparts modesty. And from modesty one gains a good position. From a good position, one earns money, and from money one can execute righteous deeds. From such deeds, one gets happiness.*

— Hitopadesha - 1.5

Herein, the poet describes very beautifully how one is benefited in stages by knowledge. Knowledge (education) imparts modesty to a person. A man who is knowledgeable develops modesty, whereas a man with half-baked knowledge becomes puffed with pride. Thus, through qualities like modesty, a man gains a good position, from which he earns well. From such money, he can serve the needy and perform good deeds. From this, he gains happiness.

12. विद्वत्वं च नृपत्वं च नैव तुल्यं कदाचन ।
स्वदेशे पूज्यते राजा विद्वान् सर्वत्र पूज्यते ॥

*Kingship and knowledge are never equal to each other. A king is respected only in his own country, whereas a scholar is respected wherever he goes.*

— Subhashita Manjari - 11.104

Kingship or ruling power and knowledge are compared here. A person can be the ruler of a small village, a state, or even a big country. But only people under his direct control respect him as a ruler. When he goes to another country or region, he is not respected in the same manner. On the other hand, a person who is very knowledgeable acquires respect wherever he goes, for knowledge is recognised everywhere.

13. विद्वानेव विजानाति विद्वज्जनपरिश्रमम् ।
न हि वन्ध्या विजानाति गुर्वीं प्रसववेदनाम् ॥

*Only a scholar can understand the nature of the efforts put in by another scholar. A childless woman cannot know the pains of delivering a child.*

— Subhashita Manjari - 11.05

The efforts put in by a scholar to become one can be appreciated only by another scholar, because he also would have put in such efforts to become a scholar. This is compared to the labour pain a woman undergoes when she gives birth to a baby. The nature of such pain remains unknown to a childless woman. Only another woman who has experienced such pains can realise it.

14. यः सततं परिपृच्छति शृणोति सन्धारयत्यनिशम् ।
    तस्य दिवाकरकिरणैर्नलिनीव विवर्धते बुद्धिः ॥

*One who frequently asks questions, listens carefully, who always recapitulates what he has learnt and makes it perfect, blooms like a lotus as the flower blooms when it comes in contact with the rays of the sun.*

— Panchatantra – 4.87

Different ways to enrich one's knowledge are described here. The process starts with asking questions and listening. One should not hesitate to ask his teacher questions, though they may seem simple or silly. In English, it is said that there are five friends of a person – the four Ws and one H, namely, What, When, Why, Where and How. If one makes use of these friends, he can learn everything about a topic. The next step will be to listen carefully to what the teacher says. One should be attentive and listen. One should analyse, recollect frequently and remember the facts. Sanskrit has three terms for this: *shravana* (hearing), *manana* (thinking), and *nidhidhyasana* (constant musing).

15. आचार्यात् पादमादत्ते पादं शिष्यः स्वमेधया ।
    कालेन पादमादत्ते पादं सब्रह्मचारिभिः ॥

*A student gains a quarter portion of knowledge from his teacher, a quarter of it from one's own intelligence, a quarter from fellow students, and a quarter from time (experience).*

— Subhashita Manjari – 11.18

This verse describes how a student can gain knowledge. He has to gain some of it from his teacher. But it is not possible to learn everything from the teacher alone. Some of it has to be learnt by oneself. Some from discussions with other students and some from the passage of time, i.e., by observation and experience.

16. रूपयौवनसंपन्ना विशालकुल संभवाः ।
विद्याहीना न शोभन्ते निर्गन्धा इव किंशुकाः ॥

*Even though a person has beauty, youth and has been born in a high family, he will not earn respect unless he has education and knowledge, just as a flower without fragrance is not admired.*

— **Subhashita Ratnavali - 2.68**

One may be very beautiful or handsome, or full of youth, vigour and strength or may be wealthy or belong to a good family and possess other qualities, but without education and knowledge all such qualities are meaningless. The poet compares this to a flower without fragrance, which though beautiful to look at, is not appreciated if devoid of fragrance.

17. सुखार्थिनः कुतो विद्या कुतो विद्यार्थिनः सुखम् ।
सुखार्थी वा त्यजेद्विद्यां विद्यार्थी वा त्यजेत्सुखम् ॥

*Where is the question of knowledge for one who is interested in pleasure? And where is the question of pleasure for a knowledge-seeking student? If one wants pleasure, he must sacrifice knowledge, and if one wants knowledge, he must sacrifice pleasure.*

— **Subhashita Ratnavali - 11.122**

Herein, there is a warning that a student interested in knowledge must forgo pleasure. For one who is lazy and a pleasure-seeker, gaining knowledge is difficult. This implies that one must desist from excessive pleasurable activities and other frivolous diversions. Recreation and entertainment should just be a part of life, not the main goal.

18. शुनः पुच्छमिव व्यर्थं जीवितं विद्यया विना।
    न गुह्यगोपने शक्तं न च दंशनिवारणे ॥

*Life without education and knowledge is waste, like the tail of a dog that is neither useful to conceal its private organs, nor useful in driving away disturbing flies.*

— Nitya Neeti - Pg. 46

Human life is most precious and one must use this in learning. The ability to think and analyse is present only in humans, not in animals. Therefore, when one is born as a human, he must acquire knowledge. Education destroys ignorance and lights the lamp of knowledge in a person. A person without education not only misuses the opportunity of human life but also wastes his energy in foolish activities that benefit neither him nor society. If he is rich, he may waste money over friends and bad habits. The poet compares such a life to a dog's curved tail, which can neither conceal its private organs, nor drive flies away. Other animals have straight tails that serve both purposes.

# Learning and Earning

19. क्षणशः कणशश्चैव विद्यामर्थं च साधयेत् ।
    क्षणत्यागे कुतो विद्या कणत्यागे कुतो धनम् ॥

*Knowledge and money should be gained using every second and every ounce of money. Where is the gain in knowledge if one loses every second of time, and where is the question of raising money if one loses an ounce of that money?*

— **Subhashita Ratnavali - 2.68**

In this verse, the poet reveals how one must build up knowledge and save money. In other words, he is trying to convey the importance of time and money. Many students do not give importance to their leisure period. They think it is not possible to learn much in a short span of time and thus waste it. But this should not be done. Every second is precious. Even a second of leisure time can be utilised effectively for learning. Such precious time, if lost, cannot be regained. Hence it is said: "Time and tide wait for none."

Similarly, many of us think that small amounts of money are of no use. But even small saving go to make a big sum. It is well said: "Every drop of water in an ocean counts." Thus, every second of time and every ounce of money should be well utilised.

20. अजरामरणवत् प्राज्ञो विद्यामर्थं च साधयेत् ।
    गृहीत इव केशेषु मृत्युना धर्ममाचरेत् ॥

*One must gain knowledge and earn money thinking that he will never die or grow old. Simultaneously, one must perform righteous deeds thinking that death is holding his hair.*

— Subhashita Manjari - 10.3

The poet beautifully describes how one must always keep learning and earning money, while simultaneously performing righteous deeds. Prophet Muhammad says, "Seek knowledge from cradle to grave." One must learn from birth right up to death. Generally, people learn up to a certain stage in life. For example, until they graduate or get a good job and then they forget learning. Others are satisfied when they earn enough to lead a simple life. That should not be the case. One should keep learning and earning irrespective of age. Knowledge is useful at any age. Likewise, one should earn money by rightful means and always seek the right means to earn more money. And one should not rest just because he gets older but always work to earn his own keep.

At the same time, one should keep doing righteous deeds, like helping the poor and needy, donating money to orphanages, reading sacred books etc, as if on the verge of death. People think that righteous or religious activities should be performed in old age so that when they die they reach heaven! The poet says that one should always think death is behind him and do good deeds. Death always comes unexpectedly. So, one should learn and earn thinking he is immortal, and do righteous deeds thinking death is always at hand.

21. जलबिन्दुनिपातेन क्रमशः पूर्यते घटः ।
    स हेतुः सर्वविद्यानां धर्मस्य च धनस्य च ॥

*A pot is gradually filled with water, as water falls into it, drop by drop. This is the way to gain all kinds of knowledge, virtue and money.*

— Hitopadesha - 2.115

The poet describes how to gain knowledge, virtue and money. It should be gradual. No man can become a millionaire or scholar overnight. It takes a couple of decades just to become a graduate! So, one must be patient with whatever he learns or earns, and be sincere in his efforts. The poet compares this to a pot filled with water. When the pot is placed under a tap, it does not get filled immediately. The water fills the pot drop by drop. The English equivalents of this verse are: "Every drop in the ocean counts" and "Rome was not built in a day". Forbearance and patience are important.

22. शनैः पन्थाः शनैः कन्याः शनैः पर्वतमस्तके ।
शनैर्विद्या शनैर्वित्तं पञ्चैतानि शनैः शनैः ॥

*The road gets trodden little by little. The cloth is woven little by little. The mountain is climbed little by little. Knowledge and money are also gained little by little. All these five are attained little by little.*

— Nitya Neeti - Pg. 93

This verse is identical to the previous one. The poet gives us more examples to say that knowledge and money are acquired gradually. As the saying goes: "The journey of a thousand miles begins with the first step."

A famous Jataka tale supports this. There was once a poor man who did not have any means of sustenance. One day, as he was going to town, he noticed a dead rat. The cashier of that town, who also saw the dead rat, told his friend that a person could make his livelihood just by that rat. The poor man overheard their conversation and picked up the rat. After a while, another man passed by with a pet cat, which looked at the rat eagerly. This man gave the poor man an anna in exchange for the rat. With that the poor man bought some jaggery and a pot of water, which he shared amongst a few flower gatherers. Pleased by this, they gave him flowers. Selling these, he bought more jaggery and water. He thus earned eight annas.

One evening he noticed that a garden had been spoilt by rain, and he told the gardener he would clean it in exchange for all the fallen wood and leaves. Distributing the jaggery to some children, he had the garden cleaned by them. He sold the wood and leaves to the king's potter as fuel for 16 annas. He then came across a team of 500 workers working in a meadow. He supplied them water and jaggery. Pleased, they offered to help him at any time. The man then befriended a sea trader, who one day informed him that a horse trader was coming to town. The man hurried to the meadow workers and asked for a bundle of grass from each one and requested them not to sell grass on that day till his stock was sold. He thus sold the grass and obtained thousand annas from the horse trader.

Next, he received information that a ship was coming to port. He dressed well and bought the ship on credit, keeping a signet ring as deposit. Many merchants who came to buy the cargo were told that the ship had been sold. So, they gave a thousand annas each to the young man for their share of the cargo! Thereby, the young man earned 100,000 annas, and went to the cashier to express his gratitude. The astonished cashier gave his daughter in marriage to the man. When the cashier died, the young man became the town's cashier!

Thus, one can improve in any field if he is sincere and perseveres. Truly is it said: "Slow and steady wins the race."

23. यस्तु संचरते देशान् यस्तु सेवेत पण्डितान् ।
    तस्य विस्तारिता बुद्धिस्तैलबिन्दुरिवाम्भसि ॥

*The intelligence of a person who travels in different countries and associates with scholars expands, just as a drop of oil expands in water.*

— **Subhashita Manjari – 11.89**

One's knowledge expands as he travels to various places, reads different books and associates with scholars. In each place, we find different kinds of people, differing histories, cultures and habits, all of which enriches a person. Likewise, our knowledge increases by understanding the views of scholars we associate with.

# Useless Knowledge and Money

24. पुस्तकस्था तु या विद्या परहस्तगतं धनम् ।
कार्यकाले समुत्पन्ने न सा विद्या न तद्धनम् ॥

*Knowledge that is only in books and money in the custody of another person, if not used at the required time, are not actually knowledge and money.*

— Subhashita Ratnavali - 16.394

This verse condemns mere accumulation of books or wealth, which are not used. We often see that some people collect a lot of books at home simply to display them and never read the books. Some read them but cannot apply the knowledge contained in them at the right time. Such an example exists in the Mahabharata. Once Drona, the teacher of the Pandavas and Kauravas, entered a river to bathe. A huge crocodile caught hold of Drona's legs, and he began shouting for help. The princes on the shore were startled, but it was only Arjuna who immediately shot several arrows and killed the beast. Thus, although everyone knew archery, only Arjuna used his knowledge when it was required. So, knowledge should not just be bookish. This applies to money too. Some people deposit money in different banks, but when it is required urgently, they can't utilise it!

25. दानं भोगो नाशस्तिस्रो गतयो भवन्ति वित्तस्य।
    यो न ददाति न भुङ्क्ते तस्य तृतीया गतिर्भवति॥

*Money has three destinies, namely, charity, self-enjoyment, and destruction. For one who neither enjoys money himself nor gives it to others, the third destiny occurs.*

— **Panchatantra - 2.157**

Money can either be used for self-enjoyment, or given in charity to help the needy. If both are not done, and it is just stored, it is eventually destroyed, either being stolen or left for someone else when the owner dies. Such a person can never be happy, and his money will be useless. As Samuel Johnson said: "A man who both spends and saves money is the happiest man, because he has both enjoyments."

# Money

26. यस्यास्ति वित्तं स नरः कुलीनः
स पण्डितः (स) श्रुतवान् गुणज्ञः ।
स एव वक्ता स च दर्शनीयः
सर्वे गुणाः काञ्चनमाश्रयन्ति ॥

*A wealthy man is indeed one of noble birth. He is a scholar, a well-informed person, and one with good qualities. He is indeed a well-spoken man and good to look at too! All qualities take the shelter of money!*

—Neeti Shataka - 39

Here, the poet ridicules the influence of money. It is well known that if a person has enough money, everyone flocks around him. All good qualities suddenly appear in him! A Yiddish proverb is an equivalent of this verse: "With money in your pocket, you are wise and handsome and you sing well too!"

27. यस्यार्थस्य मित्राणि यस्यार्थस्य बान्धवाः ।
यस्यार्थाः स पुमान् लोके यस्यार्थाः स च पण्डितः ॥

*One who has money has friends. One who has money has relatives. One who has money is indeed a man and a scholar!*

—Mahabharata - 12.8.19

An English proverb says: "Friends are aplenty when the purse is full." It is a common experience that just as ants cover a spot of sugar, friends and relatives flock around a person who has money. Says Sri Shankaracharya:

यावद्वित्तोपार्जनसक्तः तावन्निजपरिवारो रक्तः ।

"As long as a person is able to earn money, so long will the relatives be interested in him." Money is glamorous. With money, even a fool looks attractive and scholarly!

### 28. सर्वेषामेव शौचानां अर्थशौचं परं स्मृतम् ।
योऽर्थे शुचिर्हि स शुचिर्न मृद्वारि शुचिः शुचिः ॥

*Among all types of cleanliness, monetary cleanliness is the greatest. One who is clean with respect to money is indeed clean, and it is not the one clean with water and* mrittika, *a fragrant earth, who is clean.*

— Manu Smriti - 5.106

This verse appears in the *Manu Smriti*, a collection of codes of human ethics laid down by Manu, the father of mankind. Here, he says that monetary cleanliness is the most important cleanliness and thus condemns earning money by stealing or corruption. Today, there is corruption everywhere, starting from the watchman to a high-level officer. The reason for corruption is greed. The corrupt find it hard to have peace of mind, just as an unclean person is perturbed by bad odour and disease.

In earlier days, when soaps were not in use, people used a kind of fragrant earth called *mrittika* and water for bathing. The poet says cleanliness obtained by such bathing is not real cleanliness. Therefore, one should work hard and earn money, remain clean and pure in terms of money, avoid stealing and corruption by all means.

### 29. विदेशेषु धनं विद्या व्यसनेषु धनं मतिः ।
परलोके धनं धर्मः शीलं तु निखिलं धनम् ॥

*For one travelling in another country, knowledge is wealth. For one who is in difficulty, intelligence is wealth. For one who wants heaven, righteousness is wealth. Good character, however, is wealth for everyone.*

— Bharata Manjari - 13.470

The poet describes what real wealth is. It is not just money alone, and differs for different persons. For a traveller, knowledge of language and places is wealth. For a man in misery, intelligence is wealth, as with intelligence he can solve his problems. For a man who aspires for heaven after death, righteousness – charity, visiting sacred shrines, reading holy books and performing rituals and worships – is wealth. However, for all people of all ages, good character is wealth. Therefore, it is said: "If money is lost, nothing is lost, if health is lost, something is lost, but if character is lost, everything is lost." Though devoid of wealth, knowledge or education, everyone likes a person if he has noble character.

# Miser

30. कृपणेन समो दाता न भूतो न भविष्यति ।
अस्पृशन्नेव वित्तानि यः परेभ्यः प्रयच्छति ॥

*There was no man equal to a miser in generosity, and such a man won't be born in future too! It is because a miser gives away all his wealth to others without even touching it!*

— **Subhashita Manjari - 14.148**

Here, a miser is ridiculed. A miser accumulates wealth, and he neither enjoys it, nor gives it to others and, as a result, it falls into another's hands at his death. Thus the miser gives away all his wealth to others without even touching it. A generous person also gives away all his wealth! Hence, the miser is humorously called the most generous man.

31. पिपीलिकार्जितं धान्यं मक्षिकासञ्चितं मधु ।
लुब्धेन संचितं द्रव्यं समूलं च विनश्यति ॥

*Grains stored by ants, honey stored by bees, and wealth stored by a miser – all are destroyed by the roots.*

— **Subhashita Manjari - 4.542**

Here, the accumulation of excess wealth is condemned. The ants work hard and store grains, but it is destroyed. Similarly, bees collect honey from various flowers and store it, but it is stolen by animals and man, and thus destroyed. A miser's money meets a similar end. The moral is that mere accumulation of wealth does not serve any purpose but must be used to help the needy or for some other useful purpose.

# Generosity and Charity

32. तपः परं कृतयुगे त्रेतायां ज्ञानमुच्यते ।
द्वापरे यज्ञमेवाहुर्दानमेव कलौ युगे ॥

*Penance was said to be the greatest kind of righteous deed in Krita Yuga. In the Treta Yuga, it was acquisition of divine knowledge. In the Dwapara Yuga, performing sacrifices was the best one and in the present Kali Yuga, charity alone is said to be the most righteous deed.*

—Subhashita Manjari - 10.48

In the Hindu scriptures, we find that time is divided into four Yugas or periods, namely Krita, Treta, Dwapara and Kaliyuga. The present age in which we are living is called Kaliyuga or Iron Age. In this age, ill thoughts, short lifespans, diseases and many such problems perturb most people. People are beset with desires and are always busy in earning money. There is no time for people to perform righteous deeds like austere penance, sacrifices, rituals or gaining of difficult knowledge. Hence, an easier means to obtain merit to gain heaven is required. In this verse, a suitable method is prescribed for each age, and for Kaliyuga it is said to be charity.

From charity, the giver becomes happy, for he helps the one in need, and the receiver also becomes happy, for he gets rid of some difficulty. A story from the Mahabharata supports this. Once, humans, gods and demons went to Lord Brahma and asked him what would be the best means for each of them to attain merit. Lord Brahma just taught the letter द – *Da* to each one of them. The three races understood that this single letter was applicable to each one of them. The Gods understood *Da* to be दमन – *Daman*, which means "control of senses". Since the Gods live in perpetual enjoyment, they ought to control their senses and desires for self-realisation. The demons understood it as दया – *Daya* or "mercy". Since the demons are cruel to everyone, they ought to have mercy. Now, the humans remained. They understood *Da* as *Daan* or "charity", since human beings are predominantly greedy, but gain merit when they are charitable to others.

33. दातृत्वमेव सर्वेभ्यो गुणेभ्यो भासतेतराम् ।
ज्ञातृत्वसहितं तच्चेत्सुवर्णस्येव सौरभम् ॥

*Among all good qualities, charity outshines others. If it is associated with knowledge, it looks like gold with fragrance.*

—Subhashita Manjari – 10.59

The quality of charity is glorified here. When charity is associated with knowledge, it is more beautiful. And what is that knowledge? It is the knowledge that whatever a person has belongs to God, and all people are God's creations. When a person gives charity, he should never pride himself on his meritorious deed, for if he becomes proud and boasts he loses all the merit gained. Such a person won't be liked by anyone.

In the Upanishads it is stated: श्रिया देयं ह्रिया देयं श्रद्धया देयं अश्रद्धया अदेयं । "Give in plenty, give with happiness, give with interest; do not give without interest." Thus, one should give in the proper way. The Katha Upanishad cites the example of Nachiketa, the son of Vajashravas. Sage Vajashravas once performed a sacrifice and gave away some cattle as charity to Brahmins. These cows were old and feeble, however. Young Nachiketa requested his father to give healthy and young cows instead. When the father did not heed his words, Nachiketa asked Vajashravas to give him away in charity too. Enraged, Vajashravas gave away the boy to Lord Yama, the God of Death! Nachiketa, however, learnt the knowledge of the Self for Yama and returned. The Upanishads thus teach us the proper way of charity. Once a thing has been given away, it should not be taken back.

34. गौरवं प्राप्यते दानान्नतु वित्तस्य सञ्चयात् ।
स्थितिरुच्चैः पयोदानां पयोधीनामधः स्थितिः ॥

*One earns respect by being generous, not by accumulating wealth. This is why the clouds that give water are situated high, whereas the sea that receives water is located below.*

—Subhashita Manjari - 14.159

Here, the poet has very beautifully compared the giver and the receiver to clouds and the sea. The clouds that give water to the earth in the form of rain are highly respected and situated on top, while the sea that accumulates water is situated in a low position. Another example is that of the tap, which is in a higher position, while the bucket that receives the water is under the tap. In essence, a generous person is respected, while a miser is not.

35. अन्नदानं परं दानं विद्यादानमतः परम् ।
अन्नेन क्षणिका तृप्तिः यावज्जीवं च विद्यया ॥

*The giving of food is a great form of charity. But the giving of knowledge is still greater, for food provides temporary satisfaction, while knowledge gives life-long happiness.*

—Subhashita Ratnavali - 2.80

In this verse, two types of charities are mentioned. Among various types of charity, like wealth, animals, clothes etc, the charity of food is great, because it satisfies a person's hunger. But more than that is the charity of knowledge, because knowledge lasts for an entire lifespan. Teaching is a great charity and teachers are to be always revered. Knowledge dispels all forms of disbelief and superstitions.

36. दुर्भिक्षे चान्नदातारं सुभिक्षे च हिरण्यदम् ।
भये चाभयदातारं स्वर्गेऽपि बहुमन्यते ॥

*In charity when a person gives food during famine, gold (wealth) when there is prosperity, and courage at the time of fear, he earns respect even in heaven.*

—Suktimala - 332

This verse describes what to give at a particular time. Food at the time of famine, wealth during prosperity, and courage at the time of fear fetch a person much respect. Our scriptures give many examples of people who won fame on earth and in the other world too. Karna was one such hero, who gave away his divine armour and earrings, which were his means of protection.

The King Shibi was another such hero, who was once tested by Indra and Agni, who came in the form of a hawk and a pigeon. The hawk was chasing the pigeon to devour it, and the pigeon sought shelter with Shibi, who displayed great courage. In order to save the pigeon, he took the weight of the bird and offered the same quantity of his flesh to the hawk! Pleased by his act, the Gods healed his wounds. All such generous people are respected on earth as well as in heaven.

37. हस्तस्य भूषणं दानं सत्यं कण्ठस्य भूषणम् ।
श्रोत्रस्य भूषणं शास्त्रं भूषणैः किं प्रयोजनम् ॥

*The hands are decorated by charity. Truth decorates the neck (voice). The hearing of scriptures decorates the ears. So, what is the use of other decorations?*

— **Subhashita Ratnavali - 11.269**

Everyone is fond of decorating his body with various ornaments. Hands are decorated with bangles, ears with earrings, and the neck with a necklace. The poet says these are merely artificial decorations that are of no use. The real decorations are charity for the hands, speaking the truth for the neck (voice), and the hearing of moral sayings in the scriptures for the ears.

# Useless Charity

38. वृथा वृष्टिः समुद्रेषु वृथा तृप्तस्य भोजनम् ।
वृथा दानं समर्थस्य वृथा दीपो दिवापि च ॥

*It is of no use if it rains in the sea. It is of no use if a well-fed person is given food. It is of no use to give charity to a rich man. It is of no use to light a lamp when there is abundant sunlight.*

— Subhashita Ratna Samucchaya - 1.4

Many people give charity to gain fame, giving to well-to-do people. This is condemned, and the poet supports this with very good examples like rain in the sea, which is already filled with water, feeding one who has already eaten, and lighting a lamp in daylight.

# Rich and Poor

39. अहो नु कष्टं सततं प्रवासस्ततोऽति कष्टः परगेहवासः ।
कष्टाधिका नीचजनस्य सेवा ततोऽति कष्टा धनहीनता च ॥

*It is very difficult to keep travelling always. To stay at another's home is more difficult. To serve people inferior to one is even more difficult. And to remain a penniless poor man is the most difficult.*

— **Subhashita Ratnavali - 3.89**

The poet describes the difficult aspects of life. The first one is to always travel. In a government occupation or a business, one will have to keep travelling often. Much difficulty is experienced when one stays at another person's home, where he has no freedom and has to acclimatise to the latter's habits, however disagreeable. This happens when a student or an employee goes to another place and stays as a paying guest. The host may be quarrelsome, a drunkard or of a lower status, but in his home, one has to bear his arrogance patiently and do his bidding. And to remain poor is the most difficult task, for then one cannot enjoy life in any manner. Hence, one must work hard to earn money and enjoy life.

40. यस्यास्ति लक्ष्मीर्विनयो न तत्र
अभ्यागतो यत्र न तत्र लक्ष्मीः ।
उभौ च तौ यत्र न तत्र लक्ष्मीः
नैकत्र सर्वो गुणसन्निपातः ॥

*Where there is wealth, modesty is lacking. When guests visit frequently, wealth is lacking. Both (guests and modesty) are seen frequently where there is impoverishment. All qualities do not exist in one place.*

— Suktimala - 470

It is very difficult to find a person who is rich, and at the same time generous, modest, and helpful. This verse says that the rich are generally not modest. This is generally true since the rich get everything they desire from childhood itself, and do not know the real value of anything. As the scholar Katherine White Horn has said: "The easiest way for your children to learn about money is for you not to have any." It is the poor who know the true value of money; hence they usually remain modest and serve their guests with whatever they have.

41. धर्माय यशसेऽर्थाय कामाय स्वजनाय च ।
पंचधा विभजन् वित्तमिहामुत्र च मोदते ॥

*One should use his wealth in these five ways – For righteous deeds, to gain fame, to save money, to fulfil desires, and for one's relatives and friends.*

— Bhagavata - 8.19.37

Here, how a person must use his wealth is explained. All the wealth must not be stored, but spent in various ways – for righteous purposes, to perform holy activities in temples, for gaining fame, in charity, to fulfil one's desires, on one's friends and relatives, and also to save and increase it.

42. परस्परविरोधिन्योरेकसंश्रयदुर्लभम् ।
संगतं श्रीसरस्वत्योर्भूतयेऽस्तु सदा सताम् ॥

*It is very difficult for Lakshmi (wealth) and Saraswati (knowledge) to stay together. I do pray, let them always stay together with scholars.*

— Vikramorvasheeya - 5.24

It is common experience that scholars are generally poor, and the rich generally lack knowledge. Wealth and knowledge are indicated herein by their respective embodiment of Goddesses, namely Lakshmi and Saraswati. This is only due to the nature of people. Scholars seeking knowledge usually don't accord much importance to money. They value knowledge more and money is secondary for them. The rich, on the other hand, do not hanker for knowledge, as they find money is able to meet all their requirements.

But the poet says that both knowledge and money are required. A story goes that once Raman – the poet at King Krishnadevaraya's court – prayed to Goddess Kali. She appeared and showed him two cups, one with milk and the other, curd. She asked him to drink either one of them, so that he would be bestowed with knowledge or wealth. The clever Raman quickly snatched both cups and within a wink of an eye, he drank both! He then requested the goddess to excuse him, as both were important! The goddess was pleased with his quick thinking.

43. वनानि दहतो वह्नेः सखा भवति मारुतः ।
स एव दीपनाशाय कृशे कस्यास्ति सौहृदम् ॥

*The wind becomes friendly with the fire that burns the woods. But the same wind extinguishes the fire in a small lamp! Who will be friendly with the poor?*

— Panchatantra – 4.27

When a forest fire breaks out, the wind helps in spreading the fire fast, and thus befriends it. But the same wind blows out the feeble fire in a lamp. The poet compares this to the rich and poor, and says that if one is poor, no one befriends him. The suggestion is to be strong enough to stand on one's own feet.

44. संपदो हि मनुष्याणां गन्धर्वनगरोपमाः ।
दृश्यमानाः क्षणेनैव भवन्ति न भवन्ति च ॥

*The richness of men is just like a city of fairies, conjured in the clouds. As it appears, so is it lost in a second!*

— Subhashita Sudhanidhi – 162

The richness of man is compared to the city of Gandharvas – celestial fairies. This is an imaginary world seen in the screen of clouds during sunset. Such cities, although they appear very glamorous, can disappear quickly. Similarly, the wealth of a man that appears so beautiful can be lost within a second. Thieves may steal it, or fire may burn it, or the rich man can himself squander it on bad habits like alcohol, friends, women, and gambling. The friends and relatives he trusts may gradually usurp his wealth! The great saint Sri Shankaracharya said: मा कुरु धनजनयौवनगर्वं हरति निमेषात् कालः सर्वम् This means: "Do not get puffed up with pride due to the possession of wealth, people and youth. Time takes them all away in a minute!"

Thus, one should not bank too much on wealth, and be very proud of riches.

# Arts

45. साहित्यसङ्गीतकलाविहीनः साक्षात्पशुः पुच्छविषाणहीनः ।
    तृणं न खादन्नपि जीवमानस्तद्भागधेयं परमं पशूनाम् ॥

*A person devoid of interest in music, literature and arts is indeed an animal without horns and tail! It is a great fortune to animals that he lives without eating grass!*

—Neeti Shataka - 12

The poet highlights the greatness of arts in this verse and says that a person who has no interest in any of the arts, like music, literature, painting, dance etc is like an animal without horns and tail, i.e., not refined in personality. Art indicates civilisation. Jawaharlal Nehru has said: "Art is a faithful mirror of the life and civilisation of a period." Every country and every civilisation has developed its art, and the study of these different arts itself is very fascinating. Music is, in fact, the most beautiful art, for it engages one in deep concentration.

Music is actually a type of meditation and breathing exercise done in a sweeter way. One can exhibit devotion to God best through music by singing devotional songs. A great devotee of Lord Vishnu, Sage Narada is, in fact, a singer. Many saints like Purandaradasa, Tyagaraja, Ramadasa and Chaitanya took to music and literature to spread the message of the Upanishads and devotion. Music and literature are compared to the two breasts of Goddess Saraswati (सङ्गीतमपि साहित्यं सरस्वत्या स्तनद्वयम्). Just as a mother's breast milk nourishes the baby, music and literature nourish the mind by giving good thoughts.

46. आपत्कालोपयुक्तासु कलासु स्यात् कृतश्रमः ।
नृत्तवृत्तिर्विराटस्य किरीटी भवनेऽभवत् ॥

*Man should learn arts, which come into use at times of difficulty. Consider Arjuna, who joined Virata's palace as a dance teacher.*

— Nitya Neeti - Pg. 53

Defeated in the game of dice at the hands of the Kauravas, the Pandavas went into exile for 12 years. After the period of exile, they had to live for one year in disguise. During the exile, Arjuna performed penance and visited *Indra Loka* (heaven), in order to obtain different kinds of weapons from Lord Indra. At that time, he learnt music and dance from Indra's friend Chitrasena. When the exile was over, each one of the Pandavas went to King Virata's palace in disguise to join some profession. According to the rules of the game, if the Kauravas identified them during this period, they would once again have to go into 12-year exile. Arjuna disguised himself as a female dance teacher and taught dance to Virata's daughter and her friends. Thus, the learning of music and dance when he was in heaven helped him in difficulty.

By citing this example from the Mahabharata, the poet says that everyone should learn some kind of art apart from regular professional or academic studies, which is useful in times of difficulty, for instance, when one is jobless for some time. Arjuna has been called *Kiriti* in this verse, which is an epithet. The curse was a boon in disguise that helped avoid detection during the period of *ajnata vasa*.

# Occupation

47. अश्वस्य लक्षणं वेगो मदो मातङ्गलक्षणम् ।
    चातुर्यं लक्षणं नार्या उद्योगः पुरुषलक्षणम् ॥

*Speed is the characteristic feature of a horse. Intoxication is the characteristic feature of an elephant. Skill is the characteristic feature of a woman. Occupation is the characteristic feature of a man.*

— Suktimala - 293

The poet mentions speed and intoxication as the distinctive features of a horse and an elephant. Similarly, women have particular skills as a special feature, and men tend to be engaged in some occupation. Skilful tasks that need patience are more suited to women, like managing the house, taking care of children, arts like music, dance, literature, painting etc. And manual jobs involving physical and mental strength and long hours and labour befit men. Men and women should engage in some good occupation, for it keeps the house running and helps in spending time usefully. Hence it is said: "Absence of occupation is not rest; a vacant mind is a mind in distress."

48. उद्योगिनं पुरुषसिंहमुपैति लक्ष्मीः
    दैवेन देयमिति कापुरुषा वदन्ति ।
    दैवं निहत्य कुरु पौरुषमात्मशक्त्या
    यत्ने कृते यदि न सिद्ध्यति कोऽत्र दोषः ॥

*Wealth reaches the lion among men, who engages himself in an occupation. Only cowards talk of divine help. Forget divine help and work with confidence. Even then if you do not achieve results, what is your fault?*

—Hitopadesha – 1.22

The poet says that one who works sincerely easily acquires wealth. Sincere efforts definitely produce good results. But some people believe that everything is acquired by luck and worshipping the Gods without making efforts. The poet condemns this.

A story from the Mahabharata illustrates this. Once there lived two friends, Raibhya and Bharadwaja. Raibhya had two children while Bharadwaja had one called Yavakreeta. Raibhya's two children studied hard for many years and mastered the Vedas. They were well respected by everyone. Yavakreeta did not study anything and hence gained no respect. He then became jealous of the two brothers and decided to master the Vedas through penance. He performed a severe penance invoking Lord Indra. When Indra appeared, Yavakreeta asked for mastery of the Vedas as benediction. Indra advised him to study the Vedas under the guidance of a teacher, as none could master them through a boon. Indra asked him to stop the penance and disappeared.

Yavakreeta did not agree and continued his penance. Indra then came disguised as an old, feeble man and began building a sand dam over the river Ganges. Seeing this foolish act, Yavakreeta laughed at him. The old man then retorted: "When you can master the Vedas simply through penance, why cannot I build a dam out of sand?" Yavakreeta realised that the old man was Indra himself and accepted his mistake. Which is why it is said that God helps those who help themselves.

49. उद्यमः साहसं धैर्यं बुद्धिः शक्तिः पराक्रमः ।
षडेते यत्र वर्तन्ते तत्र देवः सहायकृत् ॥

*God helps one who has these six qualities: industriousness, an adventurous spirit, courage, intelligence, strength and heroism.*

—Subhashita Ratnavali – 7.162

The poet says that God himself helps one who is courageous, intelligent, adventurous, heroic and industrious. Aesop's famous fable illustrates this. A lazy farmer was once driving his wagon across a muddy road and the wheels got stuck in the earth. The farmer stepped out of the wagon and prayed to God to extricate the wheels. Nothing happened. He then put his shoulder to each wheel to extricate them partly. When he was thus struggling, God appeared and helped him extricate the wheels fully. Truly, God helps those who help themselves.

50. न लभन्ते विनोद्योगं जन्तवः संपदां पदम् ।
सुराः क्षीरोदविक्षोभमनुभूयामृतं पपुः ॥

*Living entities won't acquire wealth without working. The Gods got a chance to drink the nectar only because they churned the milky ocean.*

— Subhashita Ratnavali - 7.162

The poet cites an example to say that one has to work in order to gain anything. Even animals and birds have to move about hunting for food. In the *Bhagavad Gita*, Lord Krishna says it is the nature of everyone to work and none can sit idle even for a second.

Therefore, one should work in earnest to achieve results. The Gods and demons had frequent fights and in order to recover their power and wealth, the Gods prayed to Lord Vishnu. Lord Vishnu advised them to churn the milky ocean along with the demons and drink the nectar that arose from it. Accordingly, the Gods reached an agreement with the demons, kept the Mandara Mountain in the sea as the churning stick, tied the huge serpent Vasuki over it and holding the serpent at both ends churned the ocean. Though they faced many difficulties, they continued churning till they received the nectar. Lord Vishnu appeared as an enchanting damsel, fooled the demons and ensured only the Gods drank the nectar.

This example teaches us the importance of work. As Swami Vivekananda said: "Arise, awake and stop not till the goal is reached."

# Endeavour

51. उद्यमेन हि सिद्ध्यन्ति कार्याणि न मनोरथैः ।
न हि सुप्तस्य सिंहस्य प्रविशन्ति मुखे मृगाः ॥

*It is only by earnest endeavour that one's tasks get accomplished, not just by planning. No deer enters the mouth of a sleeping lion!*

— Panchatantra - 2.138

We all like to be great and for that we attempt big tasks. We plan very well mentally, but when it comes to performance, many of us fail. This is due to lack of hard work. Success in any task or field requires sincere effort and perseverance. Hence it is said: "No pain, no gain." The poet compares this to a lion. Though it is the king of the forest, it still has to hunt for food. No animal walks up to the lion. Likewise, despite our intelligence, we must make honest efforts to succeed.

52. यस्य कृत्यं न विघ्नन्ति शीतमुष्णं भयं रतिः ।
समृद्धिरसमृद्धिर्वा स वै पण्डित उच्यते ॥

*One whose task is never hindered by cold, heat, fear, love, prosperity or lack of prosperity is really said to be intelligent.*

— Mahabharata - 5.33.20

When we attempt a task, for example, studying for examinations, we face several hurdles that appear to hinder us from completing the task. This verse says that an intelligent person never quits due to any difficulty.

The story of King Bhageeratha supports this. This king was told that he had to bring the sacred river Ganga from heaven to earth, and have it flow over the ashes of his dead uncles, in order to gain liberation for them. So, he performed severe penance to please Lord Brahma, who agreed to his request and sent the river down. Ganga came down in a torrent and was about to wash away the earth, when Lord Shiva prevented this by binding the river in his matted hair! Bhageeratha propitiated the Lord and he let the river flow slowly. The river followed him, but on the way it swept away a sage's hermitage. In a fit of rage, the sage drank the entire river! The poor king propitiated the sage too, and he also let the river out through his ears! The king finally succeeded in bringing the river over his uncle's ashes. Thus, the intelligent one completes his task and reaches the goal, despite hindrances.

# Enthusiasm

53. उत्साहसंपन्नमदीर्घसूत्रं क्रियाविधिज्ञं व्यसनेष्वसक्तम् ।
शूरं कृतज्ञं दृढ़सौहृदं च लक्ष्मीः स्वयं याति निवासहेतोः ॥

*The goddess Lakshmi (wealth) comes all by herself to stay in a person who is enthusiastic, not lazy, knows how to work, one who is uninterested in bad habits, heroic, service-minded and very friendly.*

— Hitopadesha - 1.135

Herein, the qualities of a person who becomes wealthy are listed. Such a person is always enthusiastic to work, knows how he can accomplish a task, and never wastes time in being lazy or never wastes money on bad habits. He is always helpful and friendly towards everyone.

54. उत्साहो बलवान्नायो नास्त्युत्साहात्परं बलम् ।
उत्साहारंभमात्रेण जायन्ते सर्वसंपदः ॥

*Enthusiasm is very strong and always right. There is no strength beyond enthusiasm. If one starts a task with enthusiasm, all riches are available to him.*

— Suktimala - 425

The importance of enthusiasm is stressed. One needs to be very enthusiastic and ambitious to achieve anything in life and make honest endeavours. People who are enthusiastic never find any work difficult. A boy who likes to play never feels play is uninteresting or tiring. If he has the same enthusiasm and interest in studies, he can do wonders. Thus, if the work of a man becomes interesting, like a game, he can achieve wonders. There are very few, however, who are settled in the field of their own interest. One should develop interest in one's work to gain good results.

### 55. निरुत्साहस्य दीनस्य शोकपर्याकुलात्मनः ।
### स्वार्था ह्यवसीदन्ति व्यसनं चाधिगच्छति ॥

*For one who does not have enthusiasm, and who is pessimistic and sorrowful, all tasks are destroyed, and he becomes depressed.*

—Suktimala - 428

The plight of people who lose enthusiasm is described. One must never lose enthusiasm under any circumstances. Failures are common in everyone's life, and one should enhance efforts in all future attempts. As the saying goes: "Failure is a stepping stone to success." If one loses interest, it becomes very difficult to work further, and he ends up sorrowful.

### 56. काष्ठादग्निर्जायते मथ्यमानात्
### भूमिस्तोयं खन्यमाना ददाति ।
### सोत्साहानां नास्त्यसाध्यं नराणां
### मार्गारब्धाः सर्वयत्नाः फलन्ति ॥

*Fire springs by rubbing wooden sticks, and water springs by digging the earth. Nothing is impossible for people who have enthusiasm. Endeavours in the proper direction surely bring success.*

—Pratijnaa Yougandha Rayana - 1.18

Through any kind of difficulty, the optimistic succeed. The Pandavas are a perfect example. The Pandavas had to undergo many torments at the hands of their cousins, the Kauravas, but they never lost enthusiasm and finally regained their kingdom. An English saying goes: "The optimist sees an opportunity in every calamity, a pessimist sees a calamity in every opportunity." Likewise, an optimist sees the rose, not the thorns, while the pessimist sees the thorns and is oblivious of the rose. Thus, one should always have an optimistic outlook.

# Laziness

57. अलसस्य कुतो विद्या अविद्यस्य कुतो धनम् ।
अधनस्य कुतो मित्रं अमित्रस्य कुतः सुखम् ॥

*Where is the question of knowledge for one who is lazy? Where is the question of money for one without knowledge? Who befriends one who is without money? Where is happiness when one is friendless?*

—Subhashita Ratnavali - 2.64

Laziness is said to be the root cause of sorrow. For one who is lazy, nothing is achievable. He does not study well and because he lacks study and knowledge, he cannot earn money or make friends. The famous tale of the ants and the cricket illustrates this. The cricket being playful and lazy always spent time eating and merrymaking, while the ants worked hard and collected grains for a rainy day. When the monsoon arrived, there was no food and the cricket had to fast and suffer, while the ants fed on the stored grains and lived happily. Thus, one must not be lazy.

58. योजनानां सहस्रं तु शनैर्याति पिपीलिका ।
अगच्छन्चैनतेयोऽपि पदमेकं न गच्छति ॥

*Even though ants move slowly, they can travel up to thousand miles. But even an eagle, if it does not move, cannot step a foot ahead.*

—Subhashita Manjari - 7.97

The poet compares human nature to an ant and an eagle. Even though very small, slow moving and seemingly insignificant, the ant can advance several miles if it moves continuously. But an eagle cannot move a step without flapping its wings. There are many who are strong, talented, and intelligent, but do not achieve good results due to their laziness.

On the other hand, even a less intelligent person can succeed if he puts in continuous and sincere efforts. The story of the hare and the tortoise illustrates this. Though swift, the hare slept on the way, while a race was on with the tortoise. The tortoise moved non-stop and won the race. It is truly said: "Slow and steady wins the race."

59. रात्रिर्गमिष्यति भविष्यति सुप्रभातं
भास्वानुदेष्यति हसिष्यति पङ्कजश्रीः ।
इत्थं विचिन्तयति कोशगते द्विरेफे
हा हन्त हन्त नलिनीं गज उज्जहार ॥

*A bee entered a lotus and thought, "The night will get over. The sun will arise and bloom this flower, then I can easily get out." It then slept in the bud. Alas! An elephant came, plucked the bud and crushed it!*

— **Subhashita Manjari – 7.100**

The poet illustrates the ill effects of laziness. Here, a bee that could have easily come out of the lotus bud by biting its way through became lazy and thought that it could come out in the morning when the sun would bloom the flower. But an elephant came and destroyed the bud along with the bee. Therefore, one should never be lazy.

In Sanskrit, there is a saying: आलस्यं अमृतं विषं । "If one is lazy, even nectar turns into poison!" When one is given nectar, he may feel lazy and keep it aside thinking that he will drink it later. But by then the nectar might turn into poison and the person loses the golden chance to have nectar. This applies to any opportunity we get in life, which we should use immediately.

60. श्वः कार्यमद्य कुर्वीत पूर्वाह्नेचापराह्निकम् ।
    न हि प्रतीक्षते मृत्युः कृतमस्य न वा कृतम् ॥

*The work kept for tomorrow should be completed today itself. The work kept pending for the afternoon should be done at the beginning of the day itself. Death does not see whether we have completed a task or not.*

— **Subhashita Ratnavali - 7.160**

This verse says that no work should be kept pending, but finished as soon as possible. Death is uncertain and does not wait for a person to finish his task. If a person dies without completing the task, he cannot do it again. Death can also be taken as time. If precious time is lost, we cannot regain it. Hence it is said: "Time and tide wait for no one." This verse specifically applies to students preparing for an examination. A student may think that the day of examination is far off and waste his time. When the day of examination approaches, it won't be possible to complete all the studies in time. So, one should be very regular in work. William Stake has said: "Think in the morning, act in the noon, eat in the evening, and sleep in the night."

61. आलस्यं हि मनुष्याणां शरीरस्थो महान् रिपुः ।
    नास्त्युद्यमसमो बन्धुः कुर्वाणो नावसीदति ॥

*Laziness is a great enemy of men, present in the body itself. There is no relative equal to work, and one who keeps working never gets lost.*

— **Neeti Shataka - 3**

The poet calls laziness an enemy present in one's body itself! One may not have an enemy outside, but he forgets to recognise invisible enemies inside. Laziness is one such enemy, and its ill effects have been already explained in previous verses. On the other hand, work is said to be the best option as it brings money, health, joy and useful spending of time. Hence it is said: "Work is worship."

62. प्रथमे नार्जिता विद्या द्वितीये नार्जितं धनम् ।
    तृतीये नार्जितं पुण्यं चतुर्थे किं करिष्यसि ॥

*What can you do in the fourth part of your life, when you have not gained knowledge in the first part, money in the second part, and merit in the third part?*

—Subhashita Manjari – 14.265

This verse implies that one must work to gain knowledge, money and merit when he has enough strength. The first part of life, childhood, should be used effectively to gain knowledge. The second, youth, should be utilised for earning money, and the third, old age, should be utilised for practising religious activities. Accordingly, in the Hindu tradition, life has to be spent in four stages or ashramas – *brahmacharya* or celibacy (student), *grihastha* (householder), *vanaprastha* (hermit), and the *sannyasi* (renounced order of life). But if one wastes time in laziness, he cannot do anything at the end of his life. When he is strong, a wise person engages his useful time in gaining knowledge and money and in performing religious and righteous acts.

# Action and Divinity

63. कर्मण्येवाधिकारस्ते मा फलेषु कदाचन ।
    मा कर्मफलहेतुर्भूः मा ते संगोऽस्त्वकर्मणि ॥

*You have the right to your duty but do not claim the right for its fruits to any of its results. Do not work for results. Do not also stay without working.*

—Bhagavad Gita - 2.47

This verse from the *Bhagavad Gita*, a part of the Mahabharata, is a conversation between Arjuna, the Pandava prince, and Lord Krishna. The latter instructs Arjuna to leave the fruits of action to Him. But the fact that one has no control over the results should not mean one stops working under the pretext of fate. If one works leaving the results to God, he neither laments nor exults over bad or good results.

64. यथा धेनुसहस्रेषु वत्सो विन्दति मातरम् ।
    तथा पुराकृतं कर्म कर्तारमनुगच्छति ॥

*As a calf recognises its mother in a group of several cows, the previously committed deeds follow their doer.*

—Panchatantra - 2.132

This verse gives the basic idea of Indian religious views. When there is a group of cows, it is difficult for us to recognise the mother cow of a particular calf, but the calf can easily recognise it. Similarly, Karma or action of past deeds follows its particular doer only. It means that being souls, we take birth again and again, and the actions of our previous births influence the good or bad results we obtain now. This can be experienced in our present life itself. We may help a person and forget the incident after a long time, but that person may remember this incident and help us at another time.

65. पलायनैर्नापयाति निश्चला भवितव्यथा ।
देहिनः पुच्छसंलीना वह्निज्वालेन पक्षिणः ॥

*The action of destiny cannot be evaded even if one flees. This is just like a bird with its tail on fire. Though it flies away, it cannot escape the effects of the fire.*

— Subhashita Manjari - 7.70

This verse says that one cannot escape the results of one's Karma, which forms his present destiny. The verse cites the example of a bird whose tail has caught fire. Wherever the bird flew, it could not escape the effects of the fire. Similarly, one cannot escape the result of past actions. Therefore, keep doing good deeds, as its immediate effect is peace of mind.

66. येषां बाहुबलं नास्ति येषां नास्ति मनोबलम् ।
तेषां चन्द्रबलं देव किं कुर्यादंबरस्थितम् ॥

*For one who does not have physical and mental strength, what good can the strength of the moon do?*

— Yashastilaka - 3.54

Many people hesitate to put proper efforts to reach a goal in the belief that the planets and Gods should give power for the fulfilment of a task, and it is only by their grace that a person can get through. This verse says that physical and mental strength are important. If one lacks these, no godly or planetary power can fulfil one's task. But an intelligent person believes in God and makes enough efforts in the proper direction and succeeds.

# Evils of Men and Women

67. षड्दोषाः पुरुषेणेह हातव्या भूतिमिच्छता ।
    निद्रा तन्द्रा भयं क्रोध आलस्यं दीर्घसूत्रता ॥

*A man who wants prosperity must give up these six negatives - sleep, drowsiness, fear, anger, laziness, and postponding.*

— Hitopadesha - 2.25

Herein, the six evils that hinder a man's progress are listed. Sleep is the foremost. All of us require sleep to refresh ourselves physically and mentally. But some people sleep too much and that leads to laziness and waste of time. Six to seven hours of sleep is adequate for everyone. Drowsiness is worse than sleep, because of which one fails to concentrate. When man has fear, he cannot achieve anything. It is said: "A coward dies daily, the brave but once." Anger spoils one's mood and interest in work. It can also damage the work being done. Laziness, working slowly and postponing tasks are the worst evils.

68. पानं दुर्जनसंसर्गः पत्या च विरहोऽटनम् ।
    स्वप्नमन्यगृहे वासः नारीणां दूषणानि षट् ॥

*Drinking alcohol, association with evil people, separation from the husband, roaming out, sleeping and staying in another's house are six evils for women.*

— Hitopadesha - 2.25

Drinking alcohol is an act of evil for both men and women, but the poet specifically names it as an evil for women. Women are naturally beautiful, and evil men always try to exploit women. Lust is common to evil men. When one consumes alcohol, it removes all inhibitions. Thus, when women drink alcohol, they become vile and easily associate with evil men, which is the second evil for them. Quarrelling due to misunderstandings is common among couples, but they must compromise and live together. Yet in today's world, we see many couples being divorced. The poet says women should not live away from their husbands. Society generally has a negative impression of such women. Roaming out too much is also not good for women, especially at night, because the problems created by evil men are more at night. Sleeping too much and staying at anyone's house is also an evil for women. The story of Sita is relevant. Though she was the purest of the pure, she had to still undergo the test of fire.

### 69. पानं स्त्री मृगया द्यूतं अर्थदूषणमेव च।
### वाग्दण्डयोश्च पारुष्यं व्यसनानि महीभुजाम् ॥

*Drinking alcohol, lust for women, hunting animals, gambling, spending money lavishly and misusing it, talking sharply and in a harsh way are the evils of kings.*

— Subhashita Manjari – 9.41

The evils listed above not only apply to kings and politicians, but to all people. Drinking alcohol and lust for women are great evils. A person intoxicated by alcohol loses his inhibitions, capacity of judgment and morality. He may commit any crime. A man who is very lusty and associates with women for lust, loses ethical and moral values. Gambling is such an evil, which brings enmity between close friends and relatives. Money that should be spent usefully or in the service of the needy, if spent lavishly, builds up arrogance. Killing of animals and eating meat reduces compassion in a person. People despise harsh and hurtful speech. If a politician has all these bad qualities, he loses his power and also an opportunity to return to power in future elections.

70. व्यसनस्य च मृत्योश्च व्यसनं कष्टमुच्यते।
व्यसन्यधोऽधो व्रजति स्वर्यात्यव्यसनी मृतः॥

*Among evil habits and death, evil habits bring more distress. A person with evil habits dies many times (has more miseries), while the other dies once, and reaches heaven.*

— **Manu Smriti - 7.53**

The poet says death is better than living with evil habits. It is a common experience that when a drunkard is told that alcohol will ruin his health and life, he asks whether a person who does not drink won't die! Human life is meant to achieve high goals, God realisation being the highest. Unfortunately, many develop evil habits and become slaves to them. Such people not only destroy their own selves, but also disturb society. St. Augustine said: "He that is good, is free, though he may be a slave; he that is evil is a slave, though he be a king." The pious don't fear death and die only once, whereas the evil live in dread of death every single day of their lives.

71. दुष्टा भार्या शठं मित्रं भृत्यश्चोत्तरदायकः।
ससर्पे च गृहे वासो मृत्युरेव न संशयः॥

*Staying in a home with an evil wife, a friend who is a cheat, and a servant who argues, no doubt, is equal to death!*

— **Garuda Purana - 1.108.25**

The poet lists out different evils that are dangerous like death. The wife, said to be a companion for life, must be loving, chaste, and one who gives good suggestions. But if she turns evil, the man's position becomes distressful. Similarly, if a friend who must be helpful in need and a servant who should be loyal turn out to be cheats, it creates a lot of distress. One can never live in a home where a snake dwells.

72. खलः सर्षपमात्राणि परच्छिद्राणि पश्यति।
आत्मनो बिल्वमात्राणि पश्यन्नपि न पश्यति ॥

*A wicked person spots the defects in others, even if it is of the measure of a mustard seed. But he does not identify his own evils, which are of the measure of a bilwa fruit, though he knows them.*

**—Nitya Neeti - Pg. 114**

It is always easy to point out the drawbacks in others. But one does not realise the drawbacks present in oneself, though he knows about them. A Kannada proverb says: "One cannot see his own back." Once, some people brought a lady who had sinned before Lord Jesus, and said that they wanted to stone her. Jesus said that he who had never sinned should cast the first stone. Remembering their sinful acts, the people left her alone. Jesus asked the lady to go in peace, telling her not to commit those sins again.

73. सूर्यं प्रति रजः क्षिप्तं स्वचक्षुषि पतिष्यति।
बुधान् प्रतिकृतावज्ञा तथा तस्य भविष्यति ॥

*Mud thrown at the Sun falls into one's own eyes. Evils directed at noble people rebound on oneself.*

**— Abhana Shatakam - 42**

One should always wish and do well to others. If evil is done unto others, it rebounds on the doer. The example of sage Durvasa in the Puranas supports this. Sage Durvasa once visited King Ambareesha's palace, was displeased with the hospitality, and created a witch to kill him. Ambareesha was a great devotee of Lord Vishnu and the Lord sent his discus for the king's protection. The discus killed the witch and then followed Durvasa to kill him. The sage fled, seeking protection in the nether world but could not gain this. Finally, obeying Lord Vishnu, he fell at Ambareesha's feet. At the request of Ambareesha, the discus left him. Thus, evils directed at noble men harms the evil-doer. Joseph Parker has said: "Never throw mud. You may miss your mark and have dirty hands."

# Merits and Demerits

74. श्लोकार्धेन प्रवक्ष्यामि यदुक्तं ग्रन्थकोटिभिः ।
 परोपकारः पुण्याय पापाय परपीडनम् ॥

*I will say what many cores of scriptures have said, in just half a verse: To serve others is meritorious, and to harm others is sinful.*

—Samayochita Padya Malika - 95

The poet summarises the entire essence of all scriptures in just half a shloka. People are always in search of how to achieve *punya*, or merit, and how to get rid of *papa*, or sin. The poet says that performing good deeds and serving others brings merit, while harming others brings sin. Jesus Christ, the spiritual teacher and founder of Christianity, would narrate many parables relating this concept. He said that serving the poor was serving God. All religious reformers have preached that one should see God in everyone and help everyone, and not harm or hate anyone. In the *Gita*, the Lord says: सर्वभूतस्थमात्मानं सर्वभूतानि चात्मनि । "See Atman, the Supreme Soul in all living beings, and see all living beings in the Supreme Soul."

75. न हि पापानि कर्माणि शुद्ध्यन्त्यनशनादिभिः ।
 सीदन्त्यनशनादेव मांसशोणितलेपनः ॥

*Just fasting cannot wash off sins. Fasting dries up flesh and blood only.*

—Mahabharata - 3.2000.102

Many people commit different sins and perform fasting and austere worship to exterminate those sins. But the Mahabharata says that fasting only dries up the flesh and blood and punishes the body, while the sinful attitude remains. The Sanskrit term for fasting is *upavaasa*, which means fasting, but it also has a deeper meaning. *Upa* means 'near', and *vaasa* means 'to live'. So, it means, 'to live near God'. For prayer and devotion to God, one should not eat heavily, for it induces sleep. Thus, *upavaasa* actually involves devotion to God by chanting His names, glorifying and thinking about Him. It is only by devotion and determination that one does not commit the sin again.

76. पुण्यस्य फलमिच्छन्ति पुण्यं नेच्छन्ति मानवाः ।
    न पापफलमिच्छन्ति पापं कुर्वन्ति यत्नतः ॥

*People like the results of punya, or merit, but never like papa. People do not like the results of papa, or sin, but commit the sins knowingly, with effort!*

— Subhashita Manjari – 14.189

This verse beautifully says that people, though interested in the results of merits, like wealth, home, happiness etc, do not like to do meritorious deeds, like giving charity and helping others. Though not interested in the results of sins, like suffering, they commit many sins knowingly, like stealing, torturing and harming others.

# Heaven and Hell

77. मनः प्रीतिकरः स्वर्गः नरकस्तद्विपर्ययः ।
नरकस्वर्गसंज्ञे वै पापपुण्ये द्विजोत्तम ॥

*That which gives happiness to the mind is heaven, and that which gives sorrow to the mind is hell. The synonyms for heaven and hell are merit and sin, O best of Brahmins!*

— **Vishnu Purana - 2.6.44**

This verse from Vishnu Purana says that heaven and hell can be seen here itself, on the earth, and one need not have to die and find them in the skies later. That which gives happiness to the mind is heaven, and *punya* or merit is said to be synonymous with heaven. *Punya* involves service and sacrifice. Thus, righteous deeds, service and loving all constitute heavenly joy. Similarly, that which brings sorrow to the mind is hell, and it is called *papa* or sin, which involves harming, hating, and quarrelling with others. These acts make the mind restless, sorrowful and jealous, which is hell (painful).

78. आरोग्यं दृढगात्रत्वं आनृण्यं अघमोचनम् ।
अपारवश्यं निश्चिन्त्यं आस्तिक्यं स्वर्ग एव च ॥

*Having good health and a well-built body, having no debts, being free from sins, not being in others' control, having peace of mind, and faith in God constitute heaven itself!*

— **Nitya Neeti - Pg. 69**

Heaven can be enjoyed on earth itself when some attributes are present in a person. Health and a good body are the most important, for it is only with good health that one can do anything. Kahlil Gibran has said: "God made our bodies temples of our souls, and they should be kept strong and clean to be worthy of the deity that occupies them." Similarly, the Upanishads say: देहो देवालयः प्रोक्तः जीवो देवः सनातनः । "The body is said to be a temple, and the soul is the God eternal." Thus, the body should be kept in good condition, which helps in service, knowledge, and worship. One should work hard, earn well, and be content. One who borrows a lot of money loses peace of mind. To be free from sins, one should devote some time for prayer and reading of the scriptures, which direct one in the right way. Performing cheap tasks brings sorrow. One must have faith in God, which imparts courage and removes fear. When one has all these qualities, he enjoys happiness akin to heaven.

### 79. त्रिविधं नरकस्येदं द्वारं नाशनमात्मनः । कामः क्रोधस्तथा लोभस्तस्मादेतत्त्रयं त्यजेत् ॥

*The gates of hell are three: desire, anger, and covetousness. These three destroy the soul. Therefore, these three must be abandoned.*

— Bhagavad Gita - 16.21

The gates of hell are on earth itself, and they are desire or lust, anger, and covetousness, as described by Lord Krishna in the *Gita*. The first one is desire, which is the root cause of all evils. Man first desires, and to fulfil his desire, he does all sorts of evils like stealing, murder etc. When he cannot fulfil his desire, anger arises, and out of anger, he loses his intelligence and commits crimes. When one becomes very rich, he stores his money without spending it or giving it to anyone. He gradually develops fear for the loss of wealth, and gets mad when he loses it. Thus, a man with desire, anger and covetousness faces all sorts of difficulties and virtually lives in hell.

80. स्वर्गापवर्गयोः पुंसां रसानां भुवि संपदाम् ।
सर्वासामपि सिद्धीनां मूलं तच्चरणार्चनम् ॥

*The worship of the lotus feet of God is the basis for gaining heaven, liberation, all kinds of wealth and achievements, for humans on this earth.*

— Bhagavata - 10.18.19

God's grace is necessary to gain anything in this world like wealth, achievements, heaven and liberation. The best example for this is Sudama, who was a very poor Brahmin. He was a great devotee and childhood friend of Lord Krishna. He and his family had to starve many times, due to poverty. One day, his wife persuaded him to go to Lord Krishna and ask for some wealth. Sudama agreed, and having nothing to take as a gift just took a small quantity of parched rice for the Lord. The Lord was overjoyed to see his friend and treated him very lavishly. He enjoyed the parched rice. Sudama did not ask Him anything, nor did Krishna give him anything. But when Sudama returned to his home, he saw a magnificent palace in place of his old hut. Thus, by the grace of Lord Krishna, Sudama became very rich. But he remained as humble and devoted as before. Thus, the worship of God's lotus feet brings prosperity to the devotee.

# Righteousness

81. धृतिः क्षमा दमोऽस्तेयं शौचमिन्द्रियनिग्रहः ।
    धीर्विद्या सत्यमक्रोधो दशकं धर्मलक्षणम् ॥

*Contentedness, patience, self-restraint, not stealing, cleanliness, control of the senses, intellect, knowledge of scriptures, truthfulness, having no anger – these constitute the ten features of righteousness.*

— Manu Smriti - 6.92

This verse from the Manu Smriti – the book containing codes of proper living – describes the ten simple features of *dharma* or righteousness. Many of us wonder what exactly righteousness is. This verse defines it in simple language. One should always be contented with his earnings and not be greedy. Sri Shankaracharya rightly says: यल्लभसे निजकर्मोपात्तं वित्तं तेन विनोदय चित्तम् । "Be happy in mind with whatever money you get from the right task."

One must be patient. Many people do not tolerate others' achievements and keep trying to pull others down. One should remain patient towards others' harsh words or deeds and forgive them. A person should tame his mind to control desires, anger, jealousy and other negative feelings and employ self-restraint. One should not steal another's property or be corrupted to fulfil desires. One must keep his body and mind clean by regular bathing and good thoughts. One should read the scriptures and good books and build up his intellect, remain truthful and give up anger. Thus, one can remain righteous.

82. धर्म एव हतो हन्ति धर्मो रक्षति रक्षितः।
तस्माद्धर्मो न हन्तव्यो मा नो धर्मो हतोऽवधीत् ॥

*Righteousness kills one if he kills it. Righteousness protects one who protects it. Therefore, we should not kill righteousness and let us not get killed by the righteousness.*

— **Manu Smriti - 8.15**

The importance of being righteous is stressed. If we remain bad, the world remains bad to us, and vice versa. The world is just like a mirror – the image in the mirror laughs if the person laughs, and cries if the person cries. Similarly, the world responds the way a person behaves.

The story of the pigeon and the ant may be recalled here. A pigeon once rescued a drowning ant with the help of a leaf. On another occasion, the ant noticed a hunter aiming at the bird to kill it and bit his leg. The hunter missed his aim and the bird escaped. The Lord says in the *Bhagavad Gita*: स्वल्पमप्यस्य धर्मस्य त्रायते महतो भयात्। "Even a small amount of righteous deeds protects one from great danger."

83. धर्मादर्थः प्रभवते धर्मात् प्रभवते सुखम्।
धर्मेण लभते सर्वं धर्मसारमिदं जगत् ॥

*From righteousness, money is gained. From righteousness, happiness is gained. Thus, from righteousness everything is gained. The whole world is sustained by righteousness.*

— **Ramayana - 2.9.30**

By working in a righteous way, one earns money, which gives him peace and happiness. On the other hand, earning by unfair means, like stealing, smuggling and corruption, ensure one loses peace of mind and always remains in a state of fear, worrying about being detected. If such people increase, the world cannot exist peacefully. Therefore, righteous people sustain the world. The Sanskrit word for righteousness is *Dharma*, and it is derived from the root धृ. .. धारणे... *by sustaining*. It is said in the Mahabharata, धारण गद्धर्ममुच्यते: Dharma is called so, as it sustains the people. Thus, people can live well if they are righteous.

84. न हायनैर्न पलितैः न वित्तेन न बन्धुभिः ।
ऋषयश्चक्रिरे धर्मं योऽनूचानः स नो महान् ॥

*One does not become great by age, grey hairs, wealth, or by acquiring many relatives. The saints become great by practising righteous deeds. One who studies the scriptures is great.*

— Manu Smriti - 2.154

Many people have the wrong notion that old people are highly knowledgeable and wealthy people are highly respectable. This verse clarifies that one who is righteous is indeed great. There are many examples of this in the scriptures and history. The stories of Dhruva and Prahlada are very famous. Both were lads five years of age, and yet they were great devotees of Lord Vishnu, and achieved the highest, i.e., God realisation, which even some great yogis have failed to achieve. Likewise, Sri Shankaracharya, Madhwa, Ramanuja, Chaitanya, Swami Vivekananda and many more great people had mastered the scriptures at a young age. These people gave the world outstanding contributions, which one cannot give just by virtue of old age.

There is a Sanskrit saying: बालादपि ग्रहीतव्यं युक्तमुक्तं मनीषिभिः । "Learned men should accept words of wisdom even if it is spoken by a child."

85. धर्मो यो बाधते धर्मं न स धर्मः कुधर्मकः ।
अविरोधात्तु धर्मस्य स धर्मः सत्यविक्रम ॥

*Dharma, if it harms another's Dharma, is not Dharma, but Adharma. The Dharma that does not oppose another's Dharma is the real Dharma.*

— Suktimala - 233

All over the world there are many religions, like Hinduism, Islam, Christianity, Buddhism, Jainism, Sikhism etc. When one studies the scriptures of all these religions, and analyses their message, one is convinced that all religions have the same message. The perfect example of this in the present times was Sri Ramakrishna Paramahamsa. He studied different scriptures and practised the way of living in different religions and was convinced that all messages were the same. Unfortunately, since time immemorial there have been fights between different religions. People of each religion think their religion is greater and all other religions are false. For centuries, there have been quarrels between two communities in India and there have been cases of forcible conversions. But everyone is free to follow any religion and there should not be any force. Thus, this verse says that Dharma should not harm others.

86. महता पुण्ययोगेन मानुषं जन्म लभ्यते ।
तत्राप्य न कृतो धर्मः कीदृशं हि मयाकृतम् ॥

*It is by great merit that one gets human life. Even after getting it, Dharma was not praised. Alas! What did I do?*

— Garuda Purana – 2.24

A soul thinks in the above way at the end of his life as a human, in the *Garuda Purana*. According to our scriptures, every living being is a soul, which passes through various lives to get a human life finally. It is said that there are 8,40,000 species of living beings and the soul passes through all these bodies before getting a human life. It is through great merit and luck that one is born a human being. For it is in the human life that one has intelligence and the capacity to judge right and wrong. Therefore, after obtaining human life, one should not waste time like animals, but learn the scriptures and be righteous. A Sanskrit saying goes thus:

आहारनिद्राभयमैथुनं च सामान्यमेतत् पशुभिर्नराणाम् ।
धर्मो हि तेषामधिको विशेषः धर्मेण हीनाः पशुभिः समानाः ॥

"Food, sleep, fear, and sex are common to both animals and humans. However, Dharma is a specialty in humans, and one who is devoid of Dharma is akin to animals."

It is a common experience that animals and men have common requirements like food, sleep, sex and defence. Both can fulfil these requirements without anyone's teaching. But animals stop at that. For example, birds build nests, and spiders weave webs. But they can only go up to that task. But humans can progress further and achieve wonders. Dharma, being the greatest achievement, is therefore prescribed for humans.

87. यदा यदा हि धर्मस्य ग्लानिर्भवति भारत।
अभ्युत्थानमधर्मस्य तदात्मानं सृजाम्यहम् ॥

*Whenever righteousness gets subdued, and injustice prevails, I manifest Myself, O Scion of Bharata!*

— **Bhagavad Gita – 4.7**

This is a statement made by Lord Krishna. The Lord says that whenever there is damage to Dharma, He comes to uplift it. Once, a great demon called Hiranyakashiyapu troubled the three worlds including his pious son Prahlada, and the Lord came as Narasimha or the Man-Lion and saved the world. Similarly, He incarnated as Rama and Krishna. It is not that the Lord Himself has to come always, in His divine form. He also sends His devotees and speaks through them. Thus, in every part of the world, an incarnation occurs, to direct people in the right way. Shankaracharya, Chaitanya Mahaprabhu, Tukaram, Lord Jesus, all are examples of such incarnations. They appear when Dharma is at stake, to revive it.

# Truth

88. सत्यमेव जयते नानृतं
 सत्येन पन्था विततो देवयानः।
 येनाक्रमन्नृषयो ह्याप्तकामा
 यत्र तत् सत्यस्य परमं निधानम् ॥

*Truth alone wins, not the untruth. The godly path by which sages, who are self-satisfied, go to achieve the supreme destiny of truth is full of truth.*

— Mundaka Upanishad - 1.3.6

Truth is complete in itself. To achieve the Absolute Truth, or God, one needs to be truthful. Being truthful gives happiness. A person who is not truthful always remains in fear. One who is truthful may have to face several hurdles, but ultimately he succeeds in life.

The story of King Harishchandra illustrates this. King Harishchandra owed a debt to sage Vishwamitra and had to suffer a lot, like losing his kingdom, selling his own wife and serving as a watchman in a graveyard for the sake of truth. But finally, he came to know that all this was a test of the gods, and he received back his kingdom. Mahatma Gandhi was influenced by this story in childhood, and became an apostle of truth. Sri Aurobindo says: "Truth is the foundation of real spirituality and courage is its soul."

89. सत्यस्य वचनं श्रेयः सत्यादपि हितं वदेत्।
 यद्भूतहितमत्यन्तं एतत्सत्यं मतं मम ॥

*The words of truth are good. But words that bring goodness are better than truth. Those words that bring goodness to the living indeed constitute truth. This is my verdict.*

—Mahabharata - 12.329.13

This verse implies that truth is good, but that which bestows good on a living being is better than truth, and that itself is also truth. In other words, it says that for the sake of good if a false statement has to be made, it can be made. This can be illustrated by a story. An incident appears in the Mahabharata, where Lord Krishna Himself suggests in the midst of war that King Yudhisthira say that Dronacharya's son has been killed. Thus, untruth can be spoken if it is for the good of society.

90. सत्यं ब्रूयात् प्रियं ब्रूयात्
    न ब्रूयात् सत्यमप्रियम् ।
    प्रियं च नानृतं ब्रूयात्
    एष धर्मः सनातनः ॥

*Truth should be spoken. Pleasing words should be spoken. Truth that is displeasing should not be spoken. Lie should not be spoken just because it is pleasing. This is an eternal ethic.*

—Manu Smriti - 4.138

This verse says that truth should be spoken, which must also be pleasing. But pleasing words, if they are untrue, should not be spoken. Sudden utterance of a harsh truth, like the demise of a loved one, to a cardiac patient may cause a shock and lead to his death. Similarly, false assurances and promises should not be made by pleasing words.

91. अश्वमेधसहस्राणि सत्यं च तुलया धृतम् ।
    अश्वमेधसहस्रस्य    सत्यमेवातिरिच्यते   ॥

*When a thousand horse-sacrifices and truth are weighed, it is found that truth exceeds the thousand sacrifices.*

—Hitopadesha - 136

The Ashwamedha yajna or horse sacrifice was a ritual in which chanting and worship was done and finally the wandering horse was sacrificed to please the gods. Kings used to perform this in the past. Before its sacrifice, the horse would be allowed to wander anywhere, as warriors followed it and kings of different territories had to pay tribute and accept the performer's sovereignty, or capture the horse when it entered their territory. Kings who captured the horse had to fight. Thus, one who performed this great sacrifice enjoyed sovereignty and gained merit as well. Herein, the greatness of truth is stressed by comparing it with the merit of thousand such sacrifices and it is said that it excels even such merits.

# Non-violence

92. अहिंसा परमो धर्मस्तथाहिंसा परं तपः ।
    अहिंसा परमं सत्यं यतो धर्मः प्रवर्तते ॥

*Non-violence is the greatest form of righteousness. Non-violence is the greatest form of penance. Non-violence is the highest truth, and righteousness is sustained by non-violence.*

—Mahabharata - 13.115.23

The greatness of non-violence is stressed here. Non-violence is one of the most important messages given by all religions. This verse is from the Mahabharata, also called the Fifth Veda due to its greatness. Similarly, the *Bhagavad Gita* classifies food into three categories: *satva*, *rajas* and *tamas*. Meat, being obtained from violence, falls in the third category. Jainism and Buddhism are especially concerned with non-violence. In Sikhism, Guru Arjun Dev compares God-lovers' diet to pearls, while that of cranes consists of frogs and fish.

Non-violence should be practised physically, orally and mentally. That is, one should not harm any living being physically, or by harsh words, or mentally.

93. सर्ववेदाभिगमनं सर्वतीर्थावगाहनम् ।
    सर्वयज्ञफलं चैव नैव तुल्यमहिंसया ॥

*Study of all the Vedas, visit to all pilgrimage centres, merit obtained by performing all sacrifices, are not equal to non-violence.*

—Suktimala - 413

Studying the Vedas, pilgrimages, performing rituals and sacrifices give a lot of merit to a person, by which one attains heaven. But herein it is said that all these cannot be equal to *ahimsa* or non-violence. In other words, one who does all the above, but is violent to others, either physically or mentally, achieves nothing. Therefore, instead of taking up tedious methods to achieve the merit, everyone should practise *ahimsa*, as preached by Buddha, Ashoka, Gandhiji, *et al.*

94. अहिंसस्य तपोऽक्षय्यमहिंस्रो यजते सदा ।
    अहिंस्रः सर्वभूतानां यथा माता तथा पिता ॥

*The penance of one who practises non-violence becomes everlasting. He always gets the merits of performing sacrifices. One who is non-violent is like a mother and father to all living beings.*

—Mahabharata – 13.117.41

*Ahimsa* or non-violence is the highest Dharma. In earlier ages, people practised severe penance and performed sacrifices. But the scriptures say that if one remains non-violent, he attains all such results. In the Vedas, animal sacrifices are recommended, and it is said that the meat of sacrificed animals can be eaten under specific circumstances. However, in Kaliyuga, the present Age, such sacrifices are not recommended, and the method prescribed by the scriptures for God realisation is chanting of His holy names. The Lord also confirms this in the *Gita* by saying: यज्ञानां जपयज्ञोऽस्मि । "Of all sacrifices, I am the chanting sacrifice." But to this day, many innocent animals are still sacrificed to propitiate the Gods. Such horrible practices should be stopped. The Manu Smriti also condemns meat eating. Thus, violence should be stopped by all means to achieve peace in the world.

# Service

95. परोपकाराय फलन्ति वृक्षाः परोपकाराय वहन्ति नद्यः ।
   परोपकाराय दुहन्ति गावः परोपकारार्थमिदं शरीरम् ॥

*It is to serve others that trees bear fruits. It is to serve others that rivers flow. It is to serve others that cows give milk. Similarly, our body is meant to serve others.*

—Trishatee Vyakhya Neeti - 61

Nature teaches us by various examples that we should serve others. Trees set one such example. They give fruits and vegetables and provide shelter to those tired of walking in the hot sun, and give good air, oxygen and cool breeze. Similarly, cows give us milk and rivers provide water. A Kannada poem says that sugarcane gives us sweet juice, though it is itself crushed and a lamp, though it burns itself, gives us light. Wilfred Grenfell has said: "The service we render to others is really the rent we pay for our room on this earth." The scriptures say that everyone is part and parcel of God, and serving anyone implies serving God Himself.

96. प्रथमवयसि पीतं तोयमल्पं स्मरन्तः
   शिरसि निहितभारा नारिकेला नराणाम् ।
   ददति जलमनल्पास्वादमाजीवितान्तं
   न हि कृतमुपकारं साधवो विस्मरन्ति ॥

*In return for a small amount of water it took, the coconut tree carries heavy coconuts on its head, and gives them a large quantity of sweet water for its entire life. In this way, noble men never forget the help done to them.*

—Subhashita Manjari - 5.91

This verse explains the nature of noble men through the example of a coconut tree. Noble men never forget the service done to them. In fact, they give much more in return for whatever they receive, just as the coconut tree gives a lot of sweet water in return for a small amount of water.

97. मूलं भुजङ्गैः शिखरं प्लवंगैः
    शाखा विहंगैः कुसुमानि भृङ्गैः ।
    श्रितं सदा चन्दनपादपस्य
    परोपकाराय सतां विभूतयः ॥

*Snakes occupy the base of a sandalwood tree and monkeys occupy its top. Birds and bees use the branches and flowers. Likewise, noble men render service to all people always.*

— Subhashita Ratnavali - 6.158

Though single, a tree serves many, like snakes, monkeys, bees and birds. Similarly, a noble man, though alone, engages his time in various services. A man can study well and work in a field, thus rendering his service in that field. He can earn well, and use some portion of it in serving the needy. If he is talented, he can also serve by contributing to literature and music in his leisure hours. He obviously has to take care of his parents and children, and he can also assist his wife with her household chores. He can give useful suggestions if and when necessary. Thus, everyone can use his time in beneficial service.

98. उपकारः परो धर्मः परार्थं कर्म नैपुणम् ।
    पात्रे दानं परः कामः परो मोक्षो वितृष्णता ॥

*To help others is a great form of righteous deed, to work for others is excellence in working. To give in charity to deserving people is real desire. To have no desires is real salvation.*

— Subhashita Manjari - 10.27

To help others is a righteous deed. Sri Shankaracharya has said: देयं दीनजनाय च वित्तम्। "Give money to the needy." It is a great service to recognise one's difficulty and render help. Work should be done without motive, like parents who care for and love their children without expecting anything in return. Such work gives real pleasure. A doctor should treat patients with the intention of curing rather than merely extracting money. One should be desirous of giving charity to the deserving and that will be a true ritual. Salvation implies having no desires.

99. परोपकारशून्यस्य धिङ्मनुष्यस्य जीवनम्।
 जीवन्तु पशवो येषां चर्माप्युपकरिष्यति ॥

*Fie upon the man who lives without helping others! Hail the animals, for they serve even after their death by their skins.*

— Subhashita Manjari - 14.274

The animals help us in various ways. The cow gives us milk, which is nature's best food. Cow dung is used as fuel. Bullocks plough fields. Dogs help in guarding our homes. Sheep give us wool, and donkeys and camels help in transport. Many animals give us useful skins even after death. When animals serve us so much, human beings should learn from them and become service-minded.

100. भवन्ति नम्रास्तरवः फलोद्गमैः
 नवांबुभिर्दूरविलंबिनो घनाः।
 अनुद्धतास्सत्पुरुषाः समृद्धिभिः
 स्वभाव एवैष परोपकारिणाम् ॥

*Trees filled with fruits bow with modesty. Clouds filled with water come closer to earth. Noble people who have wealth co-operate with others. This is the very nature of service-minded people.*

— Nitya Neeti - 25

This verse explains that service-minded persons serve people of their own accord. This is illustrated with examples of trees and clouds, which bow in modesty when filled with fruits and water respectively. Everyone should learn to be modest from these examples and help people when wealthy or capable of doing something for others.

# The Art of Speaking

101. लक्ष्मीर्वसति जिह्वाग्रे जिह्वाग्रे मित्रबान्धवाः ।
 जिह्वाग्रे बन्धनं प्राप्तं जिह्वाग्रे मरणं ध्रुवम् ॥

*Lakshmi (wealth) resides at the tip of tongue. Friends and relatives reside at the tip of the tongue. Imprisonment also resides at the tip of the tongue, and even death resides at the tip of the tongue.*

— Subhashita Manjari - 14.361

This verse beautifully relates the importance of speaking properly. The tip of the tongue implies speech. By good speech one can gain wealth and friends. Similarly, by speaking harshly, one gets imprisoned and may also embrace death! A story illustrates this: Once, the teeth and tongue had a quarrel regarding who was greater. At that time, another man came near the person whose teeth and tongue were quarrelling. The teeth said that since their number was greater, they were great. The tongue began scolding the other man with bad words. The other man was enraged and slapped the first man. Four teeth lost their hold and fell! Thus, good speech begets good while bad speech begets bad.

102. केयूरा न विभूषयन्ति पुरुषं हारा न चन्द्रोज्ज्वलाः
 न स्नानं न विलेपनं न कुसुमं नालंकृता मूर्धजाः ।
 वाण्येका समलंकरोति पुरुषं या संस्कृता धार्यते
 क्षीयन्ते खलु भूषणानि सततं वाग्भूषणं भूषणम् ॥

*Bangles, necklaces that glitter like moon, smearing of the body with sandal paste, and flowers on the hairs do not decorate one. It is only cultured speech that decorates a person. All other ornaments gradually vanish, while the ornament of speech remains eternal.*

— Neeti Shataka - 17

When a cultured man speaks, it is very nice to hear him, as it is meaningful, full of wisdom, and sweet. This verse says that ornaments do not decorate a person, but good speech does. Such speech soon attracts many friends, good jobs, and fame. In the Ramayana, when Hanuman comes to meet Lord Rama for the first time in disguise, Rama recognises him to be a great person by his beautiful speech, and tells Lakshmana about it. A Tamil proverb says: "The sprouts indicate the nature of the soil, so does softness of speech indicate a good family." Thus, speech reflects one's learning, education, family and culture. It is also said that speech is the picture of the mind.

### 103. प्रियवाक्यप्रदानेन सर्वे तुष्यन्ति जन्तवः।
### तस्मात्तदेव वक्तव्यं वचने का दरिद्रता॥

*Speaking pleasing words satisfies all living entities. Therefore, only pleasing words should be spoken. What poverty exists in speech?*

— Subhashita Manjari - 14.288

Everyone can speak. But few know the art of speaking to win anyone's heart. Samuel Johnson said: "Talking and eloquence are not the same: to speak, and to speak well, are two different things." Pleasant speech costs nothing. It just requires a good mind. When good speech alone satisfies everyone, we should learn to speak well at the very least, even if we cannot do anything else.

### 104. सुलभाः पुरुषा राजन् सततं प्रियवादिनः।
### अप्रियस्य च पथ्यस्य वक्ता श्रोता च दुर्लभाः॥

*"O King, it is very easy to find people who speak pleasantly. But it is very rare to find people who hear and speak true words though they are not pleasing to hear."*

— Ramayana - 6.16.21

This verse says that people who speak pleasantly are easily available. But those who speak true words, though they may be unpleasant, are rare. It is also difficult for people to hear them. A story from the Panchatantra illustrates this. Some monkeys were feeling very cold one night. At that time, they saw a few sparks flying around and presumed them to be a real fire. When they tried to catch the sparks to avoid the cold, an intelligent bird advised them not to do so, as it was a waste of time. When it repeated its advice, the enraged monkeys hit it repeatedly and killed it! Thus, it is difficult to hear or speak true words.

105. प्राज्ञोऽपि जल्पतां पुंसां श्रुत्वा वाचः शुभाशुभाः ।
गुणवद्वाक्यमादत्ते    हंसः    क्षीरमिवांभसः    ॥

*An intelligent person, after hearing good and bad words from speakers, accepts true words just as a swan drinks only milk though it is mixed with water.*

— Subhashita Manjari – 11.62

The world is full of different kinds of speakers. Some speak well and some speak useless words. An intelligent person hears everyone, but imbibes only the good and useful speech. It is said that when a mixture of water and milk is placed before a swan, it drinks only the milk. The intelligent man is compared to a swan here. Thus one should be a good listener and use only the good words.

106. संरोहति शरैर्विद्धं वरं परशुना हतम् ।
वा चा दुरुक्तं भीभत्सं संरोहति वाक्क्षतम् ॥

*When hurt by an arrow or cut by an axe, there may be regeneration! But the wound caused by hurtful speech doesn't heal.*

— Subhashita Manjari – 11.117

One should speak very carefully, as it creates a picture of the speaker in the listener's mind. A Kannada proverb says: "Speech once spoken is an end in itself just as a pearl, once broken, is an end in itself." If a pearl breaks, it is not possible to re-unite the pieces. Similarly, if one speaks loosely, it is very difficult to set things right. So, one should always think well before he speaks and speak in a way that doesn't hurt the listener.

### 107. अप्राप्तकालं वचनं बृहस्पतिरपि ब्रुवन् ।
### लभते बह्वज्ञानमपमानं च पुष्कलम् ॥

*Speech, if not relevant to the time, is rejected, and the speaker gets dishonoured much, even though he is Brihaspati.*

— **Panchatantra - 1.67**

One must ponder whether his speech is relevant to the time and context and then speak. Everything cannot be spoken everywhere. Philosophy cannot be spoken to fools. If not relevant, speech becomes ridiculous, although the speaker may be as intelligent as Brihaspati, who is said to be the most intelligent person, and the priest of Gods. An American proverb rightly says: "Speaking without thinking is shooting without aiming."

### 108. संपूर्णकुंभो न करोति शब्दं
### अर्धो घटो घोषमुपैति नूनम् ॥
### विद्वान्कुलीनो न करोति गर्वं
### जल्पन्ति मूढास्तु गुणैर्विहीनाः ॥

*The completely filled vessel doesn't make noise. Half-filled vessels make noise. Likewise, a learned scholar never feels pride. A person with little understanding, however, keeps talking meaninglessly.*

— **Subhashita Manjari - 14.585**

There is an English proverb: "Empty vessels make more noise", which is an equivalent of this verse. Empty or half-filled vessels make noise, while fully filled vessels don't make noise. Intelligent scholars, similarly, do not speak much, remain silent and speak only when it is necessary in a short and precise way. Fools keep speaking even when it serves no purpose, like croaking frogs.

### 109. अनुद्वेगकरं वाक्यं सत्यं प्रिय हितं च यत् ।
### स्वाध्यायाभ्यसनं चैव वाङ्मयं तप उच्यते ॥

*Speech that is not agitated, which is true, pleasing, well and based on the study of scriptures, is said to constitute vocal penance.*

— Bhagavad Gita - 17.15

In the *Gita*, the Lord says that if speech consists of all the good qualities mentioned above, it constitutes a type of penance. Thus, one need not go to the forest and perform severe penance to attain merit or liberation. One can do it by right speech itself. Study of scriptures, good books and biographies of great people, along with the practical experience of life, give one enough wisdom to speak well.

# The Intelligent and the Foolish

110. काव्यशास्त्रविनोदेन कालो गच्छति धीमताम् ।
व्यसनेन तु मूर्खाणां निद्रया कलहेन वा ॥

*The intelligent spend their time by reading poetry and scriptures and indulging in humour. Fools, on the other hand, waste time in bad habits, sleep and quarrel.*

— **Hitopadesha - 1.32**

This verse gives a picture of how the intelligent and the unintelligent make use of their time. Time is very precious, and one should never waste it. The intelligent use their time in reading good books, comprising scriptures, poetic works and biographies. Even if they sit to speak with friends, they enjoy humour and relax. Fools waste precious time in sleeping, quarrelling and bad habits like gambling, drinking etc. The use of leisure time indicates whether one is wise or unwise.

111. यस्य नास्ति स्वयं प्रज्ञा शास्त्रं तस्य करोति किम् ।
लोचनाभ्यां विहीनस्य दर्पणः किं करिष्यति ॥

*What is the use of studying the scriptures for a person who lacks sense? Of what use can a mirror be for one who lacks eyesight?*

— **Subhashita Ratnavali - 2.68**

If a blind person is given a mirror it is of no use. Similarly, a person without common sense, though well versed in the scriptures, cannot apply the knowledge properly and becomes a laughing stock. A story from the Panchatantra illustrates this. Four friends set out to acquire learning. When they met each other after a long time, three of them boasted about their learning. But the fourth had not learnt anything and kept silent. As they walked up to their village, they came across the bones of an animal. By his knowledge, the first one arranged them properly into a skeleton. The second filled it with flesh and put skin onto it. The animal turned out to be a lion! The third had learnt to bring the dead back to life. The fourth one, who had not learnt anything, warned the third friend not to bring the lion back to life. Paying no heed to his words, the third friend brought it back to life. By this time, the fourth friend had climbed up a tree. The ferocious lion ate all the three men! The sensible fourth one escaped. Thus, learning by itself is not enough. One should be wise enough to apply it correctly.

112. मूर्खेण सह संयोगो विषादपि सुदुर्जरः ।
विज्ञेन सह संयोगः सुधारससमः स्मृतः ॥

*Association with fools is more dangerous than poison. Association with the intelligent is akin to the juice of nectar.*

— **Devi Bhagavata – 1.6.5**

The poet compares friendship with fools to poison, and the company of intelligent people to nectar. The company of intelligent people brings good thoughts, knowledge, interest in studies and hard work, teaches the right way to lead a meaningful life and a lot more. Whereas association with fools makes one cultivate bad thoughts and habits, which result in waste of time and money. As a proverb goes: "It is better to have combat with sandalwood rather than play with cow dung."

113. काकः कृष्णः पिकः कृष्णः को भेदः पिककाकयोः ।
वसन्तकाले संप्राप्ते काकः काकः पिकः पिकः ॥

*The crow is black, and the nightingale is also black. What then is the difference between the two? It is at the arrival of spring that the crow is a crow and the nightingale a nightingale.*

—Subhashita Manjari - 8.71

The crow and nightingale both appear black and it is difficult to distinguish between the two. Similarly, it is difficult to distinguish between the intelligent and the unintelligent. But when spring arrives, the nightingale sings sweetly and the crow caws harshly and they are easily identified. Thus, when the test comes, their true identities are revealed. An American proverb says: "A fool is like other men as long as he is silent."

114. उपदेशो हि मूर्खाणां प्रकोपाय न शान्तये।
पयःपानं भुजङ्गानां केवलं विषवर्धनम् ॥

*Advice given to fools enrages them rather than consoling them. If serpents are fed with milk, it just increases their poison.*

—Subhashita Manjari - 14.481

It is very difficult to advise fools. They usually have their own ideas, and are enraged when sane advice is given. Here, this is compared to feeding serpents. If serpents are fed with milk, they do not become friendly. Instead, their poison increases and they may turn to bite! Thus, one must be careful in advising fools.

115. एकेन राजहंसेन या शोभा सरसोऽभवत्।
न सा बकसहस्रेण परितस्तीरवासिना ॥

*The river which gets splendour by the presence of one king swan does not benefit so by thousand cranes standing on its bank.*

—Subhashita Manjari - 14.483

The swan is such a beautiful bird that its presence imparts the river splendour. But a thousand cranes cannot achieve this. By this example, the poet is indirectly saying that the presence of one intelligent person in a family or an assembly is better than the presence of many fools. In the sky, when there is one sun, there is no need for a thousand stars.

116. शक्यो वारयितुं जलेन हुतभुक् छत्रेण सूर्या तपः
नागेन्दो निशितांकुशेन समदो दण्डेन गौर्गर्दभौ ।
व्याधिर्भैषजसंग्रहैश्च विविधैर्मन्त्रप्रयोगैर्विषं
सर्वस्यौषधमस्ति शास्त्रविहितं मूर्खस्य नास्त्यौषधम्

*It is possible to extinguish fire by water. It is possible to protect oneself from the heat of the burning sun with an umbrella. An intoxicated elephant can be controlled with a goad, and a stick can be used to control cattle and ass. Disease can be cured by medicines, and even the effects of poison can be controlled by hymns. There is a remedy or medicine for every problem, but there is no remedy to control a fool.*

—Neeti Shataka - 9

The poet Bhartrihari cites problems along with their remedies. Finally he says: मूर्खस्य नास्त्यौषधम् । "There is no remedy for fools." The fool persists with his ideas and actions, and it is very difficult to deter him. A proverb says: "The foolish and the dead alone never change their opinion."

117. मूर्खा न द्रष्टव्या द्रष्टव्याश्चेन्नतैस्तु सह तिष्ठेत्
यदि तिष्ठेन्न कथयेद्यदि कथयेन्मूर्खवत्कथयेत् ॥

*One should not visit fools. Even if one comes across a fool, one must not stay with him. Even if he happens to remain with him, one should not speak to him. Even if one speaks to him, he should speak like a fool himself.*

—Subhashita Manjari - 8.229

One should not intentionally visit a fool. If one comes across a fool, one must not stay or talk for too long, for then one unknowingly tells the fool about himself. The fool may reveal this to others causing humiliation to the first person. If one speaks in an intelligent way, the fool may argue and a quarrel may ensue. So, such fools should be spoken to like fools only.

# The Noble and the Wicked

118. सद्भिस्तु लीलया प्रोक्तं शिलालिखितमक्षरम् ।
असद्भिः शपथेनोक्तं जले लिखितमक्षरम् ॥

*The word uttered casually by the noble person is like the one inscribed on a rock. But the word uttered as an oath by the wicked is like the one inscribed on water!*

—Nitya Neeti - Pg. 91

Anything inscribed on a rock lasts long, and it is difficult to erase it. But nothing can be inscribed on water, and there is no question of its retention. The poet compares the words uttered by the noble and the wicked through these examples. Even casual utterances of the noble have so much weight, implying that they will keep their word. But the wicked, even if they promise under oath, do not keep their word. A Panchatantra story illustrates this. A tiger trapped in a cage requested a passing Brahmin to release it. It swore that it wouldn't harm him. Believing it, the Brahmin released the tiger. The next moment, the tiger tried to eat him! Luckily, a jackal that was passing by used its wit and locked up the tiger again. Thus, evil people are hard to believe.

119. दुर्जनेन समं सख्यं प्रीतिं चापि न कारयेत् ।
उष्णो दहति चांगारः शीतः कृष्णायते करम् ॥

*One should not have friendship or love with the wicked. When hot, charcoal burns the hand, and when cold, it blackens and dirties the hand.*

—Nitya Neeti - Pg. 71

Through the example of charcoal, the poet says that both enmity and friendship with the wicked is bad. A story from the Panchatantra is enlightening. An old serpent once came across a pond full of frogs. Being old and weary, it could not catch any frogs for food. So, it just remained inert for many days. The young frogs, finding it harmless, befriended it and began having jolly rides on it! The serpent gradually won the king frog's confidence, and for its sustenance it was permitted to eat a frog every week. Gradually, it ate all the frogs including the king frog! Therefore, the wicked should never be befriended.

120. दुर्जनस्य च सर्पस्य वरं सर्पो न दुर्जनः।
सर्पो दशति काले तु दुर्जनस्तु पदे पदे ॥

*Between a serpent and a wicked person, the serpent is better because it bites once. The wicked person keeps biting always.*

— Subhashita Manjari – 14.516

A serpent and a wicked man are similar in their actions, since both harm others. But the poet says the serpent is better because it bites only once. A wicked person, however, always keeps harming others. The best example is Duryodhana in the Mahabharata. He was the cousin of the Pandavas and tortured them every moment. In childhood, he poisoned Bhima. Later, he tried to burn them alive in a house of wax. They escaped. Again, he invited them for a game of dice, defeated them by cheating and exiled them into the forest. Later, he visited the forest to insult them. Likewise, the wicked keep on troubling others.

121. विद्या विवादाय धनं मदाय शक्तिः परेषां परपीडनाय।
खलस्य साधोर्विपरीतमेतत् ज्ञानाय दानाय च रक्षणाय ॥

*The wicked use their knowledge in arguments, wealth to enjoy and become intoxicated, power to harm others. In contrast, the noble use the same to build their intellect, to give charity and to protect people.*

— Subhashita Ratnavali – 4.102

It is an ancient saying that one should live like Rama and not like Ravana: रामादिवत् वर्तितव्यं न तु रावणादिवत्। Rama and Ravana are two men of contrasting characters in the Ramayana. Both had knowledge, wealth and power. Ravana had studied the Vedas, but did not have any modesty. He tried to rule the three worlds himself and used his power to harm the noble and the pious. In contrast, Rama used his power and wealth to serve the people. There are more such examples in the scriptures and history.

### 122. अमृतं किरति हिमांशुर्विषमेव फणी समुद्रिरति।
### गुणमेव वक्ति साधुर्दोषमसाधुः प्रकाशयति॥

*The moon gives nectar, while the snake gives poison. A noble man exhibits good qualities, while a wicked man exhibits bad qualities.*

— Subhashita Ratnavali - 4.135

Everyone has experienced happiness obtained from the nectarine moonlight. Everyone also knows the dangerous effects of snake poison. The moon and snake are compared to a noble and a wicked man. They express whatever they have in their minds. Thus, a noble man expresses nectarine good words, a helping hand, and service to others, while a wicked man expresses anger, jealousy, and an attitude of vindictiveness towards others.

### 123. गंगा-पापं शशी-तापं दैन्यं कल्पतरुस्तथा।
### पापं तापं च दैन्यं च घ्नन्ति सन्तो महाशयाः॥

*The scared river Ganga washes away one's sins, the moon removes one's heat, and the Kalpataru (wish-yielding tree) removes one's poverty. A noble men, however, remove all the three from one!*

— Subhashita Manjari - 5.43

All the scriptures say that when one bathes in the river Ganga, all his sins are washed away. When one stands in the moonlight, his body receives a soothing effect and the mind calms down. It is said that there is a tree called Kalpataru in heaven, which yields anything a person wishes. The poet says that all the three, however, can be obtained from a noble one. In the company of noble men, good thoughts develop, and that is enough to remove one's sins. The sweet, encouraging words of noble men also dispel one's distress. Noble men are very generous and always ready to do any service. So, they are likened to the Kalpataru tree.

124. समाजेभ्यः सुमनसां सुभाषितमयं मधु।
यावज्जीवं विचिन्वन्ति साधवो मधुपा इव ॥

*Noble men, like bees that collect honey from different flowers, collect good words from the learned for their entire life.*

— Harihara Subhashita - 2.3

The poet compares noble men to bees. The bee goes to every flower and collects honey. Likewise, noble men remain humble and gather words of wisdom from all great men to live a useful and productive life. One should follow this example, and never become proud, thinking that he knows everything. If one remains humble, he can always learn more.

125. किं कुलेनोपदिष्टेन शीलमेवात्र कारणम्।
भवन्ति सुतरां स्फीताः सुक्षेत्रे कंटकिद्रुमाः ॥

*What is the use of asking about the family? The character of a person alone is to be valued. Will not thorny bushes grow in a good field?*

— Mricchakatika - 8.29

It is a general opinion that a person who hails from a good family is a noble man, and one who is born in a poor family is not so. This is not true always, for noble men are sometimes born in low families and the wicked in high ones. Thus, one's greatness should not be judged on the basis of family, caste or birth. An example is seen in the scriptures. Prahlada, a devotee of Lord Vishnu, was born to Hiranyakashyapu, a wicked demon.

Similarly, the wicked Duryodhana was born in the great Kaurava family and brought an end to the dynasty. Therefore, a person must be respected by virtue of his good character.

126. अयं निजः परो वेति गणना लघुचेतसाम् ।
उदारचरितानां तु वसुधैव कुटुंबकम् ॥

*Mean-minded people discriminate between people as their own and others. For noble men, however, the whole world forms their family.*

—Hitopadesha - 131

Noble men are always broadminded, and they see everyone as their relatives. They do not discriminate on the basis of caste, creed, colour, status etc. They see everyone as children of God and treat all equally. The Lord says in the *Bhagavad Gita*: पण्डिताः समदर्शिनः "The wise see everyone equally." In modern times, great people like Mother Teresa and Mahatma Gandhi served the poor, including so-called untouchables and lepers.

127. आदौ चित्ते ततः काये सतां सम्पद्यते जरा ।
असतां तु पुनः काये नैव चित्ते कदाचन ॥

*Noble men first grow old with respect to intellect, and the body ages later. In the foolish and wicked, the body grows first, but the intellect never grows.*

—Panchatantra - 1.177

Noble people give first priority to learning and building their intellect. But it is not that they do not care for the body; they do give necessary importance to health and fitness. The wicked and the foolish, however, spend most of their time improving their physical strength and attractiveness. Thus, though very young, noble men usually have good knowledge, whereas the foolish and the wicked just grow old without gaining wisdom.

128. उदेति सविता ताम्रस्ताम्र एवास्तमेति च ।
सम्पत्तौ च विपत्तौ च महतामेकरूपता ॥

*The Sun is red at the time of rising, and red at the time of setting too. Similarly, noble people remain the same at the time of happiness and distress.*

— **Kavya Prakasha - 7.245**

Noble men are always of one mind. They are not fickle-minded. Happiness or distress are both treated in the same way by them. They neither get excited when there is gain, nor are they depressed when there is loss. Such a way of living gives one peace of mind, and everyone should adopt this attitude. In the *Gita*, the Lord says: सुखदुःखे समं कृत्वा लाभालाभौ जयाजयौ । "One should have equanimity in happiness or distress, victory or failure."

In the Hindu tradition, the year begins with a festival called Ugadi. The speciality of this festival is that one partakes of a mixture of neem leaves and jaggery. Neem is bitter and jaggery is sweet. Eating of this mixture is to signify that one should take happiness or distress in the same way.

129. दुर्जनस्य श्वपुच्छस्य व्यालस्योष्ट्रगलस्य च ।
न मन्त्रैनौंषधैर्वापि ऋजुता जातु जायते ॥

*A wicked man, a dog's tail, a snake, and a camel's neck cannot be straightened by any amount of hymns or by medicines!*

— **Ramayana Manjari - 6.313**

The poet compares a wicked man to a dog's tail, a snake, and a camel's neck and says that just as these cannot be straightened by any amount of efforts, a wicked man also cannot be converted into a noble man so easily. The examples cited are very appropriate. A dog's tail, a snake, and a camel's neck are curved by nature, and it is not possible to straighten them. A wicked man is also similar in nature and behaviour.

130. दुर्जनः परिहर्तव्यो विद्ययालंकृतोऽपि सन् ।
मणिना भूषितः सर्पः किमसौ न भयंकरः ॥

*A wicked man, although knowledgeable, should be abandoned. Is not the snake dangerous even if it is decorated with a jewel?*

—Neeti Shataka - 51

It is believed that some snakes have precious jewels in their heads. Decorated with jewels, such snakes look very beautiful, but they are always dangerous. A person cannot touch a snake just because it is beautiful. Similarly, many wicked people are learned. But they should be avoided because they are always dangerous. The best examples are the Rakshasas or demons. Many demons like Ravana, Hiranyakashipu and Jarasandha were learned and also happened to be devotees of Lord Shiva. But because they were wicked, they had to be punished.

131. अतिमलिने कर्तव्ये भवति खलानामतीव निपुणा धीः
तिमिरे हि कौशिकानां रूपं प्रतिपद्यते चक्षुः ॥

*The wicked have great intelligence in doing vile actions. An owl can see well in darkness, indeed!*

—Subhashita Manjari - 5.4

The poet compares the wicked to an owl here. Darkness is compared to vile actions. An owl can see properly only when it is dark, and it cannot see anything in daytime. Similarly, the wicked use their intelligence very well when they are up to vile activities, and remain dumb when it comes to noble acts.

132. दूरीकरोति कुमतिं विमलीकरोति
चेतश्चिरन्तनमघं चुलुकीकरोति
भूतेषु किञ्च करुणां बहुलीकरोति
सङ्गः सतां किमु न मङ्गलमातनोति ॥

*The company of noble men puts off bad thoughts and purifies the mind. It washes away long-accumulated sins, and inculcates mercy towards all living entities manifold. What is that which is not available in the company of a noble person?*

— Subhashita Manjari – 5.71

It is one's great fortune to be in the company of noble folk. The poet lists out the various advantages one can gain from such company. It is said that once the sages Vasistha and Vishwamitra had an argument. Vishwamitra held that penance was great, while Vasistha argued that the company of pious and noble men was greater. They went to Adishesha, a great serpent that holds the whole earth on its hood, for the verdict. Adishesha asked each one of them to hold the earth for a while. Vishwamitra used the power of his penance, but could not hold the earth. Vasistha used the effect of a half-minute company with noble men and could hold it for a long time! Vishwamitra wondered about the greatness of company with good men. Therefore, one must always associate with noble people.

# Appraisal of Good Character

133. गुणवज्जनसंसर्गाद्याति नीचोऽपि गौरवम् ।
पुष्पमालाप्रसङ्गेन सूत्रं शिरसि धार्यते ॥

*From the company of men with good qualities, even the worthless person gets respected. This is just like a thread, when present in the garland of flowers, is worn over the head.*

        **—Subhashita Ratnavali - 1.28.03**

A thread is never given much importance or is worn over the head for decoration. But when it is present along with flowers in a garland, it is also worn with the flowers. Thus, it enjoys the same respect as that of a flower. Similarly, even a worthless person is respected when in the company of great people. One should always remain in the company of noble people.

134. संपत्सु महतां चित्तं भवत्युत्पलकोमलम् ।
आपत्सु च महाशैलशिलासंघातकर्कशम् ॥

*The mind of great people becomes as soft as a lotus flower when they prosper well. The same mind becomes strong as rock at the time of distress.*

        **—Neeti Shataka - 55**

Great people have equanimity in both happiness and distress. When they prosper, they show mercy towards everyone and thus remain soft as a flower. When there is distress, they remain very patient like rocks. Rocks tolerate any amount of blows. Similarly, great people tolerate any amount of distress with patience. Another Sanskrit saying which supports this idea says:

वज्रादपि कठोराणि मृदूनि कुसुमादपि।
लोकोत्तराणां चेतांसि को हि विज्ञातुमर्हति ॥

The great people are harder than diamonds at times and softer than flowers at times. Who can understand their mind which is meant to serve the world?

135. यदि सन्ति गुणाः पुंसां विकसन्त्येव ते स्वयम्।
नहि कस्तूरिकामोदः शपथेन विभाव्यते ॥

*If there are virtuous qualities in a person, they get expressed themselves. The fragrance of Kasturi incense cannot be hidden by oath!*

— Kuvalayananda - 51

Kasturi, or musk, is a fragrance obtained from the musk deer. It is so fragrant that even if it is hidden, its fragrance is unmistakeable and anyone can identify it. Similarly, a virtuous man cannot hide his good qualities. They are expressed at the right time. Therefore, a noble man need not put in effort to promote his qualities.

136. न जातिर्न कुलं तात न स्वाध्यायो न च श्रुतम्।
कारणानि द्विजत्वस्य वृत्तमेव हि कारणम् ॥

*It is good character which makes one a Brahmin. It is not caste, family, birth, studies and learning, O friend!*

— Mahabharata - 3.178.16

According to all scriptures, a Brahmin is the most respectable man. Based on this idea, people born in the family of Brahmins are usually full of pride, and generally look down upon other men. This was common in the earlier days. But the Mahabharata clarifies that respect is gained only by one's good conduct, not by one's birth and studies. King Yudhishthira also says that even a shudra who has good conduct must be highly respected, while a Brahmin with bad conduct must not be respected. One must be respected by virtue of his good character, not by virtue of birth or studies.

### 137. शैले शैले न माणिक्यं मौक्तिकं न गजे गजे।
### साधवो न हि सर्वत्र चन्दनं न वने वने ॥

*One cannot find a jewel in every mountain. One cannot find a pearl in every elephant. Holy men are not to be found everywhere, just as sandalwood cannot be found in every forest.*

— Subhashita Manjari – 14.393

Precious jewels are found in mountains. But it is not so in the case of every mountain. There was also a belief that some rare elephants had pearls over their heads. Sandal trees are seen only in few forests. Similarly, holy men are encountered rarely. When one happens to meet such holy men, one should make the best use of the opportunity to learn the noble way of life. Such people also show the pathway to God, and a means to put an end to all miseries and sufferings of the birth and death cycle.

### 138. मनसि वचसि काये पुण्यपीयूषपूर्णाः
### त्रिभुवनमुपकारश्रेणिभिः प्रीणयन्तः।
### परगुणपरमाणून्पर्वतीकृत्य नित्यं
### निजहृदि विकसन्तः सन्ति सन्तः कियन्तः ॥

*How many noble people are there who are filled with the nectar of virtues in their mind, speech and bodies; who please the three worlds by their service; who magnify the qualities of others which are very minute into mountains; and always remain happy in their hearts? (There are very few.)*

— Neeti Shataka – 55

In today's world, we find most people are selfish. But how many noble people can be found? There are very few. Here, the poet brings out the qualities of such people very nicely. Such people are full of virtues, always render service without any self-centred motives, and help others improve their good qualities. They do not do all these as a duty, but really enjoy (निजहृदि विकसन्तः) doing them. Such great souls are very rare.

The *Bhagavatam* relates a very nice story in praise of noble souls. Once the sacred river Ganga, in a depressed mood, asked the saint Narada, "O saint, lots of people bathe in my water to get rid of their sins, and I am acquiring all their sins, so how do I get rid of these sins?" The saint immediately replied, "O sacred river, when a holy person bathes in your water, you get rid of all such sins!" Such is the greatness of holy, noble men.

### 139. गुणाः सर्वत्र पूज्यन्ते पितृवंशो निरर्थकः ।
### वासुदेवं नमस्यन्ति वसुदेवं न मानवाः ॥

*One is respected by virtue of his good character, and not by virtue of his father or family. Vasudeva is not worshipped. But his son Krishna is worshipped as the Lord of beings and the world.*

— Subhashita Ratnavali - 10.185

People generally believe that they gain respect if they are from a good family or born of a great father. One need not be born into a great family or of a great father to gain respect. It is only by virtue of his character that he is respected. The poet gives the example of Krishna and his father Vasudeva. Krishna is worshipped by virtue of his qualities as the Supreme Being, but none worships Vasudev because he is Krishna's father.

### 140. साधूनां दर्शनं पुण्यं तीर्थभूता हि साधवः ।
### तीर्थं फलति कालेन सद्यः साधुसमागमः ॥

*The sight of holy men is auspicious. They are like pilgrimages personified. Pilgrimages give good results gradually, while an encounter with holy men gives such results immediately.*

— Suktimala - 153

This verse says that holy men are greater than pilgrimage centres. People generally go to pilgrimage centres to get rid of sins and to obtain merit. But the poet says this is a very gradual process, as one has to travel long distances. If one comes in contact with a holy person, knowledge, devotion and good virtues can be procured from such a person immediately, which may not even be possible by visiting pilgrimage centres. In the *Bhagavatam*, it is said that holy men sanctify even the pilgrimages by their presence (तीर्थीकुर्वन्ति तीर्थानि).

141. सदयं हृदयं यस्य भाषितं सत्यभूषितम् ।
कायः परहिते यस्य कलिस्तस्य करोति किम् ॥

*What can the vile Kali do to one whose heart is full of mercy, where speech is decorated by truth, and whose body is used to serve others?*

— Suktimala - 178

The present age is called Kaliyuga or the Age of Quarrel and the presiding person of this age is Kali, who is very vile. Kali influences everyone to build up evil thoughts and do evil actions. Here the poet questions what Kali can do to a noble man, who is always engaged in good thoughts, truthfulness, has mercy towards all living beings, and is always serving the poor and needy. Kali or any bad influence cannot harm one who is noble.

142. मनीषिणः सन्ति न ते हितैषिणः
हितैषिणः सन्ति न ते मनीषिणः ।
सुहृच्च विद्वानपि दुर्लभो नृणां
यथौषधं स्वादु हितं च दुर्लभम् ॥

*There are intelligent people who are not well-wishers. And there are well-wishers who are not intelligent. It is rare to find people who are both intelligent and friendly, just as it is difficult to find a medicine that is good for health and also sweet.*

— Subhashita Manjari - 14.555

People are generally reluctant to take medicines, especially pills, since they are bitter. But they are necessary to cure a disease and restore health. Sugar candy or any such sweets are nice to eat, but cannot be taken in large quantities, as they spoil one's health. It is difficult to find medicines that are good as well as sweet. Similarly, it is difficult to find people who are intelligent and well-wishers at the same time.

143. क्षमया दयया प्रेम्णा सूनृतेनाजवेन च ।
वशीकुर्याज्जगत्सर्वं विनयेन च सेवया ॥

*The whole world can easily be won by forgiveness, mercy, love, good words, honesty, modesty and service.*

— Suktimala - 82

The poet lists all good qualities by which the whole world can be won. The best example of this in the modern period was Mahatma Gandhi. He was born an ordinary man, but by virtue of his good qualities he became world famous and gained thousands of followers. His life was like a yogi's. Hence, he was rightly called Mahatma or a great soul. One should attempt to develop such good qualities in one's life.

144. सर्वे कङ्कणकेयूरकुण्डलप्रतिमा गुणाः ।
शीलं चाकृत्रिमं लोके लावण्यमिव भूषणम् ॥

*All qualities are artificial, like bangles, and earrings. But character is natural, like one's beauty.*

— Subhashita Manjari - 10.173

One decorates his or her body with various ornaments, like necklaces, bangles, earrings etc. All these are artificial decorations, while the beauty of a person is natural. In other words, if one is not beautiful, any decoration with ornaments isn't of much help. Likewise, good character is the natural quality of a person, while intelligence, studies, talents and wealth are artificial qualities. One who does not have good character is not respected even if he has other qualities. An American proverb says: "Character is the diamond that scratches every other stone."

145. गुणं पृच्छस्व मा रूपं शीलं पृच्छस्व मा कुलम् ।
सिद्धिं पृच्छस्व मा विद्यां भोगं पृच्छस्व मा धनम् ॥

*Ask for good qualities, not for beauty. Ask for good character, and not the family. Ask for achievements, and not the amount of studies. Ask for enjoyment, and not the wealth.*

— Suktimala - 68

Beauty is nice, but it is not eternal. One gets old and loses his beauty. But the good qualities one possesses remain long after. The family one comes from may not be a great one, but the character of the person can be good. On the other hand, one hailing from a good family may not have good character. So, one must look for character, and not for family. One might have studied more, but may not be practically interested or have the ability to work, or use and apply his knowledge well. So, achievements must be noted. One may possess lot of wealth, but he may be a miser, which serves no purpose. Thus, the poet says the qualities one actually possesses is to be given credit.

146. तृणानि भूमिरुदकं वाक्चतुर्थी च सूनृता ।
एतान्यपि सतां गेहे नोच्छिद्यन्ते कदाचन ॥

*Grass, earth, water and good words - these four are never to be found missing in the homes of noble men.*

— Mahabharata - 5.36.34

Noble men may be very poor, but they never treat any guest badly. They treat guests like God. It is said in the Upanishads: अतिथि देवो भव । "Treat your guests as God." Noble people follow this instruction strictly and the basic needs of hospitality are never missing in their homes. On the other hand, when one visits a wicked man who may be very rich, he does not even offer a seat or speak a few good words. What is the use of this richness?

147. धनिनोऽपि निरुन्मादाः युवनोऽपि न चञ्चलाः ।
    प्रभवोऽप्यप्रमत्तास्ते महामहिमशालिनः ॥

*The great noble people are not proud even if they are rich, not fickle-minded even if they are young and not intoxicated even if they are in power.*

—Subhashita Manjari – 5.73

It is a common experience that a very modest person becomes proud once he becomes rich. The youth are generally fickle-minded and cannot concentrate on one aspect. Similarly, when a person gets power, he becomes arrogant and intoxicated. An example is found in the Mahabharata. A king called Nahusha was once selected by the Gods to occupy the seat of Indra, the King of Heaven. Indra having killed a demon, who was a Brahmin's son, had fled in fear of the sin. Nahusha was at first very modest, but gradually became very proud and arrogant due to his power. The poet says here that noble people are not like this, and they remain the same even when wealthy, powerful, and young.

148. उपकारिषु यः साधुः साधुत्वे तस्य को गुणः ।
    अपकारिषु यः साधुः स साधुः सद्भिरुच्यते ॥

*What is the greatness in one being good to one who has helped him? He is the real noble man, who remains good even to those who have offended him.*

—Subhashita Manjari – 14.480

People generally help only those who help them, but noble men are merciful and good even to those who offend or harm them. The best example of this is Jesus Christ. Jesus always preached about loving even one's enemies. Even when he was being crucified, he never blamed his oppressors but instead prayed to God to forgive their sins. The theme of this verse is not to encourage the offenders, but to give them another chance to reform themselves and win their hearts through love and affection.

# Modesty

### 149. नयस्य विनयो मूलं विनयः शास्त्रनिश्चयः ।
### विनयो हीन्द्रियजयः तद्युक्तः शास्त्रमृच्छति ॥

*Modesty is the basis of morality. Modesty is to be achieved by the study of scriptures. Modesty is the victory over senses. One who is modest attains the essence of the scriptures.*

—Subhashita Sudhanidhi - Pg. 60-1

"Knowledge brings modesty" is a popular saying. This verse also says that modesty is the ultimate achievement one should gain from the study of scriptures. One who is modest is always respected and such a person has control over his senses. He wins everyone's heart. One should always remain humble and polite even though he knows a lot. In fact, one who has learnt more becomes more humble.

### 150. उपकर्तुं यथा स्वल्पः समर्थो न तथा महान् ।
### प्रायः कूपस्तृषां हन्ति सततं न तु वारिधिः ॥

*It is the humble that help but not the mighty. The well quenches one's thirst but a large ocean does not.*

—Subhashita Manjari - 14.85

One can help others if he has a good mind and is humble. A small well can quench one's thirst with its sweet water, while an ocean containing salty water cannot. Similarly, a rich person who is not humble may not help anyone. Here the question of approachability too arises. A humble person can be approached easily but not the powerful.

151. विनयो रत्नमकुटं सच्छास्त्रं मणिकुण्डले ।
त्यागश्च कङ्कणं येषां किं तेषां जडमण्डनैः ॥

*What is the necessity of artificiality for one who has modesty as the crown, study of noble scriptures as earrings, and sacrifice as the bracelet?*

— Bharata Manjari - 4.356

The poet lists essential, internal qualities and compares them favourably with external ornaments. Among them modesty is said to be the crown of all ornaments. A person can gain all good qualities by effort, like the study of good books, service-mindedness, intelligence etc, but can easily develop pride by virtue of all such qualities. But rarely do people remain humble in spite of having many good qualities. Therefore, humbleness is given prime importance. The idea is that before the crown (modesty) other ornaments are insignificant.

152. नभोभूषा पूषा कमलवनभूषा मधुकरो
वचो भूषा सत्यं वरविभवभूषा वितरणम् ।
मनोभूषा मैत्री मधुसमयभूषा मनसिजः
सदोभूषा सूक्तिः सकलगुणभूषा च विनयः ॥

*The sun is decorative to the sky. The bee is decorative to a garden of flowers; truth is decorative to speech; charity is decorative to wealth; friendship is decorative to the mind; love is decorative to the spring season; good words and proverbs are decorative to an assembly, and modesty is decorative to all qualities.*

— Suktimala - 295

The poet beautifully lists various aspects, and those that decorate them. Finally, he says that modesty decorates all qualities in a man. Thus, if one has modesty, all his other qualities shine.

# Friendship

153. केनामृतमिदं सृष्टं मित्रमित्यक्षरद्वयम् ।
आपदां च परित्राणं शोकसन्तापभेषजम् ॥

*Who created this nectarean, two-lettered word मित्र 'mitra' [friend]? It protects one who is in difficulty, and is a medicine for sorrow and distress.*

— Panchatantra - 2.62

It is a great fortune to have a good friend. A true friend is one who shares both happiness and distress. Such a person tries his best to remove his friend's distress. The duty of a friend is illustrated in the Ramayana. Lord Rama, who was in sorrow as his wife Sita was abducted by Ravana, befriended a monkey chief called Sugriva. Sugriva promised Rama that he would help find Sita if Rama would help restore his kingdom back to him. Sugriva's brother Vaali had seized Sugriva's kingdom. Rama agreed, killed Vaali and restored the kingdom to Sugriva. Sugriva then became engrossed in sensual pleasures and forgot his promise! Lakshmana, Rama's brother, and Hanuman reminded Sugriva about this, and Sugriva immediately swung into action. Thus, a friend should help at the time of distress. It is therefore said: "A friend in need is a friend indeed."

154. आपत्काले तु संप्राप्ते यन्मित्रं मित्रमेव तत् ।
वृद्धिकाले तु संप्राप्ते दुर्जनोऽपि सुहृद्भवेत् ॥

*One who is a friend at the time of difficulty is really a friend. Even a wicked man becomes one's friend at the time of prosperity.*

— Panchatantra - 2.118

This verse is similar to the previous one and says that a true friend is one who helps at the time of difficulty. When one prospers, everyone likes to be his friend, including a wicked man, for his wealth attracts everyone. But rarely do people turn up to help at the time of distress. A person should be helpful to his friend in times of prosperity and distress as well.

155. उपकाराच्च लोकानां निमित्तान्मृगपक्षिणाम् ।
भयाल्लोभाच्च मूर्खाणां मैत्री स्याद्दर्शनात्सताम् ॥

*Friendship occurs among the ordinary people by mutual help. It occurs between animals and birds on occasions. It occurs among fools by fear and covetousness. And in case of noble people, it occurs just by mutual sight.*

— Panchatantra - 2.37

The poet speaks about friendship amongst different kinds of people. Ordinary people generally make friends when some help is necessary and thus remember them. In case of animals and birds, it is occasional and they do not remain friends for long. Among fools, it is due to fear and greed. A fool makes friends with a powerful man out of fear or greed, thinking that he may be given wealth often. In case of noble people, however, just the sight of each other creates friendship between them, for their thoughts and actions are similar.

156. मृगा मृगैः सङ्गमनुव्रजन्ति
गावश्च गोभिस्तुरगास्तुरंगैः ।
मूर्खाश्च मूर्खैः सुधियः सुधीभिः
समानशीलव्यसनेषु सख्यम् ॥

*The deer make friends with deer, cattle with cattle and horses with horses. Similarly, fools befriend fools and the intelligent make friendship with the intelligent. Friendship thus occurs between people of similar character and habits.*

— Subhashita Manjari - 14.557

Singers generally like to make friendship with other singers, or those with a taste for music. People interested in sports generally like to have friends interested in sports. Similarly, people interested in studying make friends with scholars and learned people, while people with bad habits make friends with similar people. As the English proverb goes: "Birds of a feather flock together."

### 157. न मातरि न दारेषु न सोदर्ये न चात्मनि।
### विश्वासस्तादृशः पुंसां यादृङ्मित्रे स्वभावजे ॥

*The faith that men have by nature in friends is not found in their mothers, wives, brothers and themselves!*

— Hitopadesha - 2.166

A person who may not listen to the advice of his parents easily accepts the same from his close friend. This is the power of friendship! A person without confidence in himself becomes confident when encouraged by his friend. In the Ramayana, we find that Hanuman did not have confidence in his own strength, but he behaved like a powerful giant when his friend Jambavan encouraged him. The caring words of a good friend are like a powerful medicine. Hence, it is said that even a parent should behave like a friend to his son after he becomes sixteen: प्राप्ते तु षोडशे वर्षे पुत्रं मित्रवत् आचरेत्।

### 158. सन्तप्तायसि संस्थितस्य पयसो नामापि न श्रूयते
### मुक्ताकारतया तदेव नलिनीपत्रस्थितं राजते।
### स्वात्यां सागरशुक्तिमध्यपतितं तन्मौक्तिकं जायते
### प्रायेणाधममध्यमोत्तमगुणाः संसर्गतो जायते ॥

*A drop of water, when it falls on a burning iron piece, is lost nameless. The same drop of water, if it falls on a lotus leaf, looks like a pearl. And the same drop of water, if it falls through Swati rain into an oyster shell, is converted into a pearl! Similarly, whether a person becomes the lowest, intermediate or best man depends on his association.*

— Neeti Shataka - 58

The poet beautifully brings out the effects of association through the example of a drop of water. A water drop disappears when it falls on a hot burning iron piece. Similarly, if a person associates with a fool or a wicked man, he too turns out to be like that and spoils his life. If the drop of water falls on a lotus leaf, it appears like a pearl. A person associating with an ordinary but good person becomes like that. This person is the intermediate. A person associated with the best of men also turns out to be the best. It is a belief that a particular rain called Swati is special in that a drop of water in this rain falling into an oyster gets converted into a pearl. Similarly, association of a man with the best makes him likewise.

159. आरम्भगुर्वी क्षयिणी क्रमेण
लघ्वी पुरा वृद्धिमती च पश्चात् ।
दिनस्य पूर्वार्धपरार्धभिन्ना
छायेव मैत्री खलसज्जनानाम् ॥

*In the beginning of the day, the shadow [of an object] is long, and it gradually decreases in length. In the latter part of the day, the shadow, which begins short, gradually increases in length. Friendship with the wicked and noble diminishes and progresses in this way.*

— Neeti Shataka - 49

The poet explains about friendship with the wicked and the noble through the example of a shadow. Just as a shadow is longer in the morning, and gradually shortens by noon, friendship with the wicked is strong at first, but gradually diminishes. The shadow that starts as a short one in the latter part of the day increases in length gradually. Similarly, friendship with noble people is not strong in the beginning, but progresses gradually and becomes very strong.

160. विवादो धनसंबन्धो याचनं स्त्रीषु सङ्गतिः ।
आदानामग्रतः स्थानं मैत्रीभङ्गस्य हेतवः ॥

*Arguments and quarrels, money matters, begging, interest in women, getting into an exalted position – all these are causes for break in friendship.*

— Subhashita Manjari - 14.575

Close friends develop enmity by arguments and quarrels. Therefore, they should come to a compromise when arguments arise. Money and women make friends into enemies. The Panchatantra relates the story of Dharmabuddhi and Papabuddhi, who were friends, but when they earned a lot of money, the latter stole everything and blamed the former! The Puranas similarly relate the story of Sunda and Upasunda, who were close friends, and lived like two bodies and one soul. They prayed for a boon that they should die only in each other's hands. When they tormented the world, in order to put an end to them, Lord Brahma created a damsel and sent her to them. For the sake of her hand, both friends fought with each other and died. Thus, certain things are detrimental to friendship.

### 161. रहस्यभेदो याच्ञा च नैष्ठुर्यं चलचित्तता।
### क्रोधो निःसत्वता द्यूतमेतन्मित्रस्य दूषणम् ॥

*Revealing secrets, begging, being harsh, fickle-mindedness, anger, lack of virtues and gambling are the drawbacks of a friend.*

—Hitopadesha - 2.72

The poet lists the drawbacks of a friend. A friend is very close to a person, and it is natural that he knows many things about him. In the interest of friendship, one must not reveal his secrets. He should also not beg for an object very dear to his friend. He should always be sweet and humble, and not harsh and angry. He should possess good virtues, and must never gamble, as gambling can easily spoil a friendship, as illustrated in the Mahabharata, where gambling between the cousins led to a bloody war.

### 162. सार्थः प्रवसतो मित्रं भार्या मित्रं गृहे सतः।
### आतुरस्य भिषङ्मित्रं दानं मित्रं मरिष्यतः ॥

*A companion is a friend for the traveller. The wife is a friend for one who stays at home. A doctor is a friend for the diseased; and charity is a friend for one who is dying.*

—Mahabharata - 3.313.64

This verse tells us about a right friend for the right person. A companion is the friend of a traveller, for he converses with him, gives suggestions and keeps him engaged. For a householder, the wife is a friend, as she gives him love and affection. Similarly, for a diseased patient, a doctor is a friend, for he can cure him and save his life. Charity is a friend for the dying person, for it gives him fame and merit, to enjoy prosperity in heaven or the next life.

# Relatives

163. सत्यं माता पिता ज्ञानं धर्मो भ्राता दया सखा।
शान्तिः पत्नी क्षमा पुत्रः षडेते मम बान्धवाः ॥

*Truth is my mother, knowledge is my father, righteousness my brother, compassion my friend, peace my wife, forgiveness my son – these six are my relatives.*

— Nitya Neeti - Pg. 4

The poet beautifully brings out all the good qualities of a man in the form of different relatives. Relatives help a man at times of difficulty and give him happiness by sharing good thoughts and actions. Thus, one should have good relatives for prosperity. When a person possesses all these good qualities as relatives, he is sure to prosper.

164. उत्सवे व्यसने चैव दुर्भिक्षे शत्रुनिग्रहे।
राजद्वारे श्मशाने च यस्तिष्ठति स बान्धवः ॥

*A person who stands as a companion at times of prosperity, distress, famine, subduing of enemies, at the king's entrance, and in a graveyard, is a real relative.*

— Subhashita Manjari - 6.10

A relative is supposed to help one and share moments of prosperity and distress equally. The poet cites different circumstances along with prosperity, where it is very difficult for a person to manage alone. Therefore, whoever comes to help in such circumstances is to be considered and treated like a relative.

165. यः प्रीणयेत् सुचरितैः पितरं स पुत्रः
यद्भर्तुरेव हितमिच्छति तत्कलत्रम् ।
तन्मित्रमापदि सुखे च समक्रियं यत्
एतत्त्रयं जगति पुण्यकृतो लभन्ते ॥

*He who pleases his father by his good conduct is really the son. She who wishes her husband's good alone is really the wife. He is the real friend who treats his friend equally at the time of happiness and distress. Meritorious people in the world acquire these three.*

—Subhashita Trishati - 1.59

Everyone cannot be a good son just by taking birth. The poet says a good son should please his father by his good conduct. He should serve his parents, and at the same time try to win a good name in society so that the father's name is not tarnished. The Vedas and Upanishads define son as: पुन्नामनरकात्त्रायते इति पुत्रः । "He is the son or *putra*, who prevents his father from entering a hell called *pum*." By his good virtue, a son can do this. The Ramayana gives the example of Lord Rama, who was an obedient and ideal son to his father. He even went to the forest to keep his father's word. A true wife, likewise, is the one who always wishes for the good of her husband and serves him with love and affection. Such wives are called *pativrata* – devoted to the husband. And a true friend is good at the time of prosperity and distress.

166. जनिता चोपनेता च यश्च विद्यां प्रयच्छति ।
अन्नदाता भयत्राता पञ्चैते पितरः स्मृताः ॥

*One who gives birth, one who initiates, one who teaches, one who feeds, and one who protects from fear – all these five are to be treated as a father.*

—Subhashita Manjari - 13.24

The poet cites five great men who are to be given the same respect as a father. The first is the father himself. The father must be respected like God, according to Vedic injunction: पितृदेवोभव । for it is from him that one has obtained the human body, which is most precious. The next is one who initiates. Initiation or *Upanayanam* – the scared thread ceremony – is done for Brahmins, Kshatriyas and Vaishyas, in which the Gayatri mantra is taught. Such a person, who enables one to enter a spiritual life, must also be respected. The teacher, who gives us knowledge, on which is based our moral, intellectual and professional progress, must also be respected (आचार्यदेवोभव). Likewise, one who feeds at the time of hunger or famine, and one who protects a person in a fearful situation must also be respected like a father.

167. राजपत्नी गुरोः पत्नी भ्रातृपत्नी तथैव च।
पत्नीमाता स्वमाता च पञ्चैते मातरः स्मृताः ॥

*The wife of the king, the wife of the teacher, the wife of the brother, the wife's mother and one's own mother are said to be five mothers for a person.*

— Suktimala – 593

The poet mentions five persons who should be treated like a mother. It is said in the Vedas: मातृदेवोभव। "Look upon your Mother as God." An English proverb says: "God cannot be everywhere. So He created the Mother." A mother is the closest relative of a person. A mother takes a lot of pain to give birth and bring up a child. The mother also acts as the first teacher for the child. Hence, a mother must be respected. A king is said to be a representative of God, as he protects his people. So his wife also must be treated like a mother. Similarly, the brother's wife, and teacher's wife must be respected just as the brother and teacher are respected. The wife's mother, who has given her daughter in marriage to the person, is the mother-in-law and thus must be respected like one's mother.

# Courage

168. धीराः शोकं तरिष्यन्ति लभन्ते सिद्धिमुत्तमाम् ।
धीरैः संप्राप्यते लक्ष्मीः धैर्यं सर्वत्र साधनम् ॥

*The courageous one overcomes miseries, and attains good prosperity. Wealth is acquired by the courageous. Courage is indeed the means to achieve everything.*

—Subhashita Ratnavali - 19.428

One should have the will and courage to achieve anything in life. Lots of obstacles arise, but a courageous person overcomes all and finally reaches his goal. A king, who was defeated by an enemy every time they fought, got too depressed and hid himself in a cave. There he saw a spider trying in vain to climb up a wall. It tried thirty-six times, kept falling down, but succeeded in the thirty-seventh attempt. The king learnt a lesson from the spider and went into battle again with great courage. This time he won back his kingdom. One should always be courageous and he can achieve anything.

169. छिन्नोऽपि रोहति तरुः क्षीणोऽप्युपचीयते चन्द्रः ।
इति विमृशन्तः सन्तः सन्तप्यन्ते न दुःखेषु ॥

*Even a chopped tree sprouts again. Even the moon that wanes daily, waxes again. A wise and noble man thus analyses and does not get depressed in situations of difficulty.*

—Neeti Shataka - 79

Failure or sorrow is common to every man, and one should not lose heart thinking that one failure is the end of everything.

Abraham Lincoln, who was the president of the United States, is a very good example. He had many failures – he failed in business twice, was defeated in a legislative election, lost his wife, had a nervous breakdown, lost congressional and senatorial elections, failed in his effort to become vice president, but was finally elected the President of the United States! Beethoven was criticised by his teacher, who said that he could never learn music. Beethoven went on to become one of the best musicians of all time!

### 170. नाभिषेको न संस्कारः सिंहस्य क्रियते मृगैः ।
### विक्रमार्जितसत्त्वस्य स्वयमेव मृगेन्द्रता ॥

*The lion is never crowned as the king or gets trained by the animals. It gains the position of kingship by its own powers.*

—Hitopadesha - 1.16

Among all the animals, the lion is the most powerful, courageous and majestic. A single roar of the lion makes all animals tremble. Hence, it is rightly called the king of beasts. The Lord also says in the *Gita*: "Among all animals I am the lion." मृगाणां च मृगेन्द्रोऽहम् । But how did the lion gain its position? No other animals crowned it. It became the lord just by its courage and power. Anyone with courage can become a leader and he does not require any support or encouragement. But one should not use cruel means to become a leader. Only the positive aspects of the lion are to be considered here, like courage, power and majesty.

### 171. सिंहः शिशुरपि निपतति मदमलिनकपोलभित्तिषु गजेषु ।
### प्रकृतिरियं सत्त्ववतां न खलु वयस्तेजसो हेतुः ॥

*A lion, though being a young one (cub), springs up over the intoxicated temples of elephants. This is the way of virtuous people. Age is not a hindrance for power and courage.*

—Neeti Shataka - 36

Noble people indicate their future when they are young. A proverb says: "By the husk you may guess the nut." The cub of a lion, though young, attempts to fight an elephant! It does not think about its age or physical strength. It is courageous at a young age itself. We should similarly develop qualities of courage and perseverance at a young age, for then such qualities are rooted in our minds and come to the fore when we face difficulties.

172. दोषभीतेरनारम्भः कापुरुषस्य लक्षणम् ।
कैरजीर्णभिया भ्रातर्भोजनं परिहीयते ॥

*It is the feature of a coward not to begin a task fearing failure. Who has given up eating for the fear of indigestion?*

— Hitopadesha – 2.50

Every task ends up in failure or success. A courageous person does not think about the results and he takes up the task, works sincerely and succeeds. A coward worries about failure and fails to take up the task itself. Everyone eats food daily, but we occasionally suffer indigestion. But do we ever stop eating because of this? Similarly, we must work courageously without the fear of failure.

173. एकेनापि सुपुत्रेण सिंही स्वपिति निर्भयम् ।
सैव दशभिः पुत्रैर्भारं वहति गर्दभी ॥

*A lioness sleeps without fear even if it just has only one efficient cub. But an ass, though it has ten offspring, has to carry heavy weights.*

— Subhashita Manjari – 14.95

What we are ourselves may define what our offspring are. A lioness knows that if she is asleep when danger lurks, even one efficient cub will quickly growl a warning to her. But an ass with ten offspring will still have to pull her own weight. Likewise, a wise man could expect his son to act wisely in times of adversity. But a fool can expect his sons to act foolishly according to the example he has set them.

174. निन्दन्तु नीतिनिपुणा यदि वा स्तुवन्तु
लक्ष्मीः समाविशतु गच्छतु वा यथेष्टम् ।
अद्यैव वा मरणमस्तु युगान्तरे वा
न्याय्यात्पथः प्रविचलन्ति न धीराः ॥

*Courageous people never quit the path of justice, whether the wise insult or glorify them, whether wealth comes or not, whether death occurs this day itself or after an age.*

— Neeti Shataka - 81

Courageous people stick to the path of truth and justice, and never deviate from it in spite of facing many hurdles. But victory always comes to such people. The scriptures teach us to be like that citing various examples of Lord Rama, Harishchandra, King Yudhishthira, King Nala and others. All these great personalities suffered a lot to keep their promises. But they underwent all difficulties for the sake of truth and emerged victorious.

# Weakness

175. अश्वं नैव गजं नैव व्याघ्रं नैव च नैव च ।
अजामित्रं बलिं दद्यात् देवो दुर्बलघातकः ॥

*No one takes a horse, elephant or a tiger for sacrifice. The poor lamb is sacrificed. Behold, even God strikes at the weak!*

— Subhashita Manjari – 7.13

A lamb is commonly sacrificed to God, and strong animals like the horse, elephant and tiger are never used for sacrifices. The poet says that even God kills the weak! The other animals resist and defend themselves when taken for sacrifice but a lamb does not. The verse says that if one is bold and strong, everyone supports that person. If one is weak and cowardly, none comes to help. Swami Vivekananda says: "Weakness is constant strain and misery, weakness is death. Strength is felicity, life immortal. Strength is the medicine for the world's disease."

# Self-respect

176. क्षुत्क्षामोऽपि जराकृशोऽपि शिथिलप्रायोऽपि कष्टां दशा
मापन्नोऽपि विपन्नदीधितिरपि प्राणेषु नश्यत्स्वपि।
मत्तेभेन्द्रविभिन्नकुम्भपिशितग्रासैकबद्धस्पृहः
किं जीर्णं तृणमत्ति मानमहतामग्रेसरः केसरी ॥

*Will the lion, the foremost among the self-respected ones who, though weakened by hunger, old age, decreased strength, many difficulties, and with its life about to end, like to tear open the temples of an intoxicated elephant and eat the flesh or eat dried grass?*

—Neeti Shataka - 72

The poet cites the example of a lion and talks about self-respect. A lion, the most powerful of animals, likes to hunt on its own and eat. It never begs anyone or depends on mean action. Even when it is old, weary, diseased, or about to die, it does not eat grass for survival. Similarly, a man with self-respect must not become mean or adopt cheap methods like being corrupt, stealing or begging to earn a livelihood. He should work hard by any of the right means and live with honour and self-respect.

177. कुसुमस्तबकस्येव द्वे वृत्ती तु मनस्विनः।
मूर्ध्नि वा सर्वलोकस्य शीर्यते वन एव वा ॥

*A person of self-respect lives like a flower, in two ways, either getting on top of everyone's head, or ending its existence in the forest itself.*

—Neeti Shataka - 72

A flower has two alternatives in life – to decorate the head of God's statue or any person, and if that is not possible, to dry up in the forest itself. But it does not adopt any foul means to get adorned in someone's head. Similarly, self-respecting people work to their best abilities and live with whatever they earn. They do not beg or adopt foul means to gain money or popularity.

178. मनस्वी म्रियते कामं कार्पण्यं न तु गच्छति।
अपि निर्वाणमायाति नानलो याति शीततताम् ॥

*People of self-respect desire to have death rather than a humiliating life. Fire dies out but never turns cold.*

– Hitopadesha – 1.45

A self-respecting person never tolerates insults and humiliation. He is ready to accept death rather than be humiliated. Therefore, such a person lives honestly, though he may face many difficulties in such a living. The poet cites the example of fire, whose nature is to burn with heat. No one has ever heard of cold fire. Fire is always hot. It just ceases to exist rather than get cold. This is similar to self-respect.

# Mind

### 179. मनो धावति सर्वत्र मदोन्मत्तगजेन्द्रवत् ।
### ज्ञानांकुशसमा बुद्धिस्तस्य निश्चलते मनः ॥

*The mind wanders everywhere like an intoxicated elephant. Intelligence, with goad-like knowledge, stops the wandering of the mind and calms it down.*

—Nitya Neeti - Pg. 116

In the Mahabharata, when a Yaksha asked Yudhishthira what was faster than wind, he answered that it was the mind. The mind is so fast it travels miles within a second. To control such a mind is most difficult. The mind always likes to enjoy itself and forces man to use his senses to obtain enjoyment. This sense gratification gives temporary happiness and never allows contentment. As we enjoy the world more, we do so without actually achieving complete happiness. The reason is that all of us are really spirits and belong to a divine nature rather than being merely physical beings. So, when we involve ourselves in spiritual activities like meditation, chanting of God's holy names and reading the scriptures, we can control the mind. The poet compares this knowledge to *ankusha* or a goad, which is used to control intoxicated elephants. The wandering mind is compared to an intoxicated elephant, and a goad to knowledge, which can control it.

### 180. मनः प्रसादसौम्यत्वं मौनमात्मविनिग्रहः ।
### भावसंशुद्धिरित्येतत् तपो मानसमुच्यते ॥

*The peace of mind, pleasantness, silence, self-control, purity of thoughts, all these constitute mental penance.*

—Bhagavad Gita - 17.16

The scriptures say that one should be pure in mind, speech and body. In this verse, Lord Krishna explains how one can perform penance through the mind, and thus be pure. The mind should be at peace and should be pleasant. It should not get subjected to the six enemies of a person – lust, anger, covetousness, intoxication, greed and jealousy. When these are controlled, the mind achieves peace. The easiest method for this, as recommended by the scriptures, is by prayers and (कलौ तद्धरिकीर्तनम्) "Chanting God's names in Kaliyuga." One should not speak unnecessarily and foolishly. One should speak about noble matters. One should have self-control and the ability to control desire and anger. One should have good thoughts. This comes by reading holy books and through association with holy persons.

181. यथाम्भसि प्रसन्ने तु रूपं पश्यन्ति चक्षुषा ।
तद्वत्प्रसन्नेन्द्रियवान् ज्ञेयं ज्ञानेन पश्यति ॥

*As one can see his reflection in clear water, one who has a pleasant mind and senses understands the one to be understood by knowledge.*

— Nitya Neeti - Pg. 50

When water is clear, one can see his reflection in it. But if the same water is dirty, one cannot see his reflection. The poet compares the mind to water. The mind is basically clear like water. But just as the water can become impure, the mind also easily becomes impure through bad thoughts and actions. These thoughts and actions are developed through the senses: the eyes, ears, tongue, skin and nose. Sense control involves engagement of these senses in a proper way. The eyes must be engaged in seeing the good and auspicious, the nose to smell flowers offered to God, and the ears to hear about Him. The hands and legs should be used to serve people and visit temples. Marrying to beget good children can also meet the sexual urge. By all these activities the mind becomes peaceful and then it can easily think better.

In the Upanishads it is said: मन एव मनुष्याणां कारणं बन्धमोक्षयोः । "The mind alone is responsible for the bondage and liberation of human beings."

182. यत्सत्यं रमणीयानां स्वस्थे मनसि रम्यता।
अचारु सुखिनां चारु चारु दुःखाय दुःखिनाम् ॥

*When the mind is peaceful, everything appears pleasant. For the person who is happy, even the unpleasant appears pleasant. For one who is unhappy, even the pleasant looks unpleasant.*

—Ramayana Manjari – 3.1136

The human mind is very powerful. It is basically clear and we can train it the way we want. This is called *conditioning*. The famous experiment done by the scientist Pavlov illustrates this. He tied a dog, and every time he gave it food, he rang a bell. The dog would salivate when food was given and it got conditioned to the sound of the bell. One day, Pavlov just rang the bell without giving any food and the dog still salivated! We can similarly condition our mind to react to situations like anger, anxiety, fear, depression etc. Keeping the mind peaceful and calm, one can react peacefully to situations that normally provoke anger and fear. Singing devotional songs also brings about happiness. The poet says that for such a man, even the unpleasant looks pleasant. On the other hand, for an unhappy person, even the pleasant looks unpleasant. John Milton has rightly said: "The mind is in its own place, and in itself can make a heaven of hell and a hell of heaven."

183. सविता विधवति विधुरपि सवितरति
तथा     दिनन्ति    यामिन्यः।
यामिन्यन्ति    दिनानि   च
सुखदुःखवशीकृते   मनसि   ॥

*For the mind of one subject to happiness or sorrow, the sun appears like the moon, and the moon like the sun. Similarly, days appear as nights, and nights as days!*

—Suktimala – 371

This verse serves an example for the previous one. As stated before, for the happy mind even the sun appears like the cool moon, and days like cool nights. Moonlight gives coolness to everyone, but for one who is away from his beloved, the same appears hot! Thus, it is the state of mind that is important. A peaceful mind takes happiness and distress in an equal manner and does not get perturbed by either.

184. मनस्येकं वचस्येकं कर्मण्येकं महात्मनाम् ।
मनस्येकं वचस्येकं कर्मण्येकं दुरात्मनाम् ॥

*Great people have oneness in mind, speech and action. But the wicked have one thing in mind, one in speech, and another in action.*

— Subhashita Manjari - 14.552

This verse is an intelligent composition by the poet. Grossly, it appears to be saying the same with respect to both the noble and wicked. But when one reads it twice or thrice, he understands its real meaning. It says that noble people speak whatever they have in mind. They also act the way they speak. As a proverb says: "Practise what you preach." But the wicked have one thought, say something else and do another thing! For example, a wicked man may have thoughts of lust and greed. He may secretly involve himself in vile activities like drinking and smuggling without letting others know this. The poet highlights the difference between the noble and wicked in this way.

185. यथाऽऽगारं तु सुच्छत्रं वृष्टिर्न समति विध्यति ।
एवं सुभावितं चित्तं रागो न समति विध्यति ॥

*Just as rainwater does not seep into the house, which is well protected by a roof, lust and desire do not distract a well-trained peaceful mind.*

— Nitya Neeti - Pg. 150

A house should have a good roof. It is then well protected from rain. Similarly, the mind should be stable. A stable mind overcomes all desires and miseries. A man who has no distractions can concentrate and achieve wonders. This is possible for everyone. Swami Vivekananda says: "Within each one of you, there is the power to remove all wants and miseries. The powers of the mind are like the rays of the sun dissipated. When they are concentrated, they illumine. Each soul is potentially divine. The goal is to manifest this divinity within by controlling nature, external and internal. Do this either by work, worship, psychic control, or philosophy."

Lord Krishna cites the example of a tortoise in the *Gita*. He says that just as the tortoise pulls all its limbs into its shell, so should one pull his senses within from external objects. This is possible by chanting holy names or by meditating, since the human mind can attend to only one thing at a time.

186. अनवस्थितचित्तस्य सद्धर्ममविजानतः ।
परिप्लवप्रसादस्य प्रज्ञा न परिपूर्यते ॥

*The unsteady mind, not knowing about the righteous conduct of life, which is always undulating, never gets completed.*

—Nitya Neeti - Pg. 149

A mind that does not have a right goal, and doesn't know the values of life, just wanders like a mad elephant. Such a mind keeps hovering from one object of pleasure to another, without finding true happiness. But true happiness comes when one engages in his duty rightfully, lives rightfully, and dedicates his life to service. Life is always full of duality and we have to learn forbearance. Lord Krishna says in the *Gita*: "By contact with hot or cold, we too feel hot or cold. Similarly, happiness and sorrow come and go. Learn forbearance." By knowledge and righteous conduct, the mind becomes steady, peaceful and complete.

# Happiness and Sorrow

187. सर्वं परवशं दुःखं सर्वमात्मवशं सुखम् ।
 एतद्विद्यात्समासेन लक्षणं सुखदुःखयोः ॥

*To be under another's control is sorrowful and to be independent is happiness. These are in brief the features of sorrow and happiness.*

— Suktimala - 352

A person who is independent, and can do anything independently, is really happy. A dependant person who has to ask the permission of his master for every single task is sorrowful. Many times, it so happens that even learned and intelligent people have to work under people much younger in age, with lesser qualifications and knowledge. Such people, proud about their wealth and position, often treat employees like inferior beings. All this brings sorrow. Although kept in a golden cage, a parrot cannot be happy after all!

188. सुभिक्षं कृषके नित्यं नित्यं सुखमरोगिणि ।
 भार्या भर्तुः प्रिया यस्य तस्य नित्योत्सवं गृहम् ॥

*For one who works in the fields, everyday is a prosperous day. For a healthy person without any disease, everyday is a happy day. Everyday is a festive occasion in one's home, who has a loving wife.*

— Subhashita Manjari - 14.433

The ways of achieving happiness are described by the poet here. A farmer has to work hard everyday in the fields. He then gets good crops. This applies to all professions. Whatever may be one's profession, he has to put in hard efforts to get good results. One must do this with interest. A Kannada proverb says: "If the hands get soiled, the mouth is full of curd." If one puts in honest endeavour, he achieves something. For him, every day is a prosperous day. Health is the most essential possession of a person. It is said: "Health is wealth." One may have wealth and opulence, but if he has bad health, what can he enjoy? Therefore, one must protect his health. For a healthy man, every day is truly a happy day. But this is realised only when one is diseased!

For a married man, the most lovable person is his wife, and for her, the husband. If both understand each other and live peacefully without desiring much and quarrelling, they will experience a festive atmosphere everyday. Thus, one does not need opulence to be happy, but understanding and contentment.

189. सुखमापतितं सेव्यं दुःखमापतितं तथा।
चक्रवत्परिवर्तन्ते दुःखानि च सुखानि च ॥

*One must accept sorrow just as one accepts happiness. Happiness and sorrow come rotating one after the other, just like a rotating wheel.*

— Hitopadesha - 2.134

This verse explains the eternal truth of life: Happiness and sorrow come to a person like a rotating wheel. In a rotating wheel, one portion remains up, and the other remains down. The next moment, the portion that was down goes up and vice versa. Likewise, one gets happiness for some time and sorrow for some time. Our scriptures teach us this lesson through various stories about Nala, Rama, Harishchandra, Yudhishthira, Satyavaan and many others. All these great kings had to undergo sorrowful situations, but they patiently persevered with the truth and finally prospered. Likewise, we should learn to bear sorrowful situations.

190. व्यसनानन्तरं सौख्यं स्वल्पमप्यधिकं भवेत् ।
 काषायरसमासाद्य स्वाद्यतीवाम्बु विन्दते ॥

*The happiness one gets after passing through a difficult event, though little, appears to be a lot. It is like one who finds even water to be very tasty after tasting bitter food and drink.*

— Suktimala - 357

The statement given by the poet and the example in support of it are common experiences for everyone. When one exerts for some time and then rests even for a while, he feels relaxed. After studying for the whole day at school, a student plays for a while in the evening and feels joyful. A person preparing for exams finds the task very difficult, but once it is over, he is relieved and happy. Thus, one must work hard to experience rest and relaxation. If there is joy at all times, it may not be valuable. Therefore, one should not get depressed when he faces a difficult situation, for behind every difficulty there always lies happiness.

191. कस्य दोषः कुले नास्ति व्याधिना को न पीडितः ।
 व्यसनं केन न प्राप्तं कस्य सौख्यं निरन्तरम् ॥

*Is there any family without a drawback? Who is the person never affected by disease? Who is the person who has never faced any difficulty? Who has happiness at all times?*

— Suktimala - 359

Old age, disease, sorrow, and death are problems everyone faces. No one is an exception. So, when one meets a difficult situation, he should not be disappointed that he alone is put to hardship. Accepting that everyone encounters difficulty, one should face the situation boldly. The story of Gautami and Buddha illustrates this. Gautami was a poor lady who once approached Lord Buddha and requested him to bring her dead child back to life. Buddha asked her to get some mustard seeds from a house where death had never occurred. She agreed, and visited many houses, but received the reply that at least one member of the household had died in every house. She returned empty-handed to Buddha, who then explained that death befell everyone, and she should not lament over it.

Thus, difficulties and sorrows visit everyone and no one remains happy always.

192. सुखमध्ये स्थितं दुःखं दुःखमध्ये स्थितं सुखम्।
द्वयमन्योन्यसंयुक्तं प्रोच्चते जलपङ्कवत् ॥

*Amidst happiness there is sorrow, and amidst sorrow, there is happiness. Both of them remain together, just as water and mud remain together (in muddy water).*

— Suktimala - 361

In muddy water, both water and mud remain together. Similarly, happiness and sorrow are companions. One may think that marriage may ensure happiness, but this happiness is followed by many difficulties, like childbirth, bringing up the child, maintaining the family etc. One may buy a car for convenience, but then the car has to be washed, filled with costly petrol, and requires regular servicing and maintenance. Thus, every happy instance is also associated with sorrow. Therefore, one must try to find happiness in everything.

193. प्रातः स्नानं गवां सेवा आरामः पुष्पवाटिका।
मातापित्रोश्च शुश्रूषा शास्त्राय च सुखाय च ॥

*Taking bath in the morning, serving the cows, gardening, and serving parents give happiness as well as fulfilment of the word of the scriptures.*

— Suktimala - 360

There are various procedures given in the scriptures to gain merit and virtue. But many of them are very difficult to follow. So, the scriptures have also given some simple methods by which people belonging to all castes and races can gain virtue. Such methods include bathing daily, serving cows by feeding them grass and water, gardening and watering plants, so that one can use flowers and tulsi leaves to worship God, serving one's parents and pleasing them by virtuous actions, chanting God's holy names etc. By these methods one can gain happiness and also act according to the scriptures. The Lord says in the *Gita* that He will be pleased if one offers Him just a leaf, flower, some water or a fruit with devotion.

### 194. ददाति प्रतिगृह्णाति गुह्यमाख्याति पृच्छति । भुङ्क्ते भोजयते चैव षड्विधं प्रीतिलक्षणम् ॥

*Giving, taking, revealing secrets and hearing them, eating, and feeding – these six are the signs of love.*

— Panchatantra - 2.51

Six signs of love are mentioned here. The loved ones present and accept gifts as a token of friendship and love at different occasions like birthdays, wedding anniversaries etc. The gift may be a high-priced one or a low-priced one. But when it is given with love any gift pleases the receiver. Friends and lovers and husbands and wives share all the secrets they know, which is also a sign of love. The loved ones should eat together and feed each other when they visit one another. When all members of a family sit together and eat, it brings happiness. Also, when the food is limited, sharing makes bonds stronger.

### 195. आपत्सु मित्रं जानीयात् युद्धे शूरं धने शुचिम् । भार्या क्षीणेषु वित्तेषु व्यसनेषु च बान्धवान् ॥

*A friend is known at the time of difficulty. A warrior is known in a battle, a clean person is known with respect to money, a wife is known when the husband is lacking money, and relatives are known at the time of distress.*

— Hitopadesha - 2.54

The poet explains how the true love of a person can be known. A person will have many friends, but most of them enjoy his company only when he is prosperous. When he is in difficulty, only the true friend comes to his help. Many warriors boast about their powers, but a true warrior is recognised only in the battlefield. There is a relevant example in the Mahabharata, where a prince named Uttarakumara kept boasting about his love for battle. But when a battle really took place and he was asked to fight, he gave various reasons to keep away from the fighting. Finally Arjuna, who was disguised as a female dancer, took him to battle. At the sight of the Kaurava army, Uttara trembled and tried to flee.

Similarly, a person who loves to be clean and pure can be tested with respect to money. A truly pious person is never attracted to corrupt means. A wife may behave lovingly with her husband, but her true love is tested only when he is penniless.

# Beauty

196. किमप्यस्ति स्वभावेन सुन्दरं वाप्यसुन्दरम् ।
 यदेव रोचते यस्मै भवेत्तत्तस्य सुन्दरम् ॥

*Is there anything that can be considered beautiful or not beautiful by nature? Whatever a person likes is said to be beautiful by him.*

– Hitopadesha - 1.46

In nature, every flower, plant, tree and animal and every human are beautiful in their own way. Everyone has different tastes. For instance, some may like the colour orange, some yellow and others red. There is a Sanskrit proverb that says: "Taste differs from person to person." One cannot force another to like whatever he likes. But the liking of one person should not harm the other. Another proverb says, "Beauty is in the eyes of the beholder."

197. रमणीयः स हि पुरुषो रमणी यत्रैव रंजति विदग्धा ।
 श्लोकः स एव सुभगश्चित्तं सक्तं हि यत्र रसिकस्य ॥

*He is really an attractive and handsome person in whom a well-learned lady finds appreciation. That is really a poem that attracts the mind of an elegant person.*

– Vishwagunaadarsha - 317

This verse speaks about real beauty. Real beauty is present in one who possesses wisdom so that a well-learned lady appreciates him. The story of King Solomon is enlightening. Solomon was a very wise king. The Queen of Sheba, who was also very wise, once came to test him. She held two similar bouquets of flowers before him. One was made from artificial flowers. She asked him to identify the real flowers. Solomon asked that the windows be opened, whereupon the bees came in. The bees hovered over both flowers and then settled over the real ones. The Queen of Sheba appreciated Solomon's intelligence. Similarly, a poem or verse is said to be beautiful if it attracts a wise person.

198. शीलभारवती कान्ता पुष्पभारवती लता।
अर्थभारवती वाणी भजते कामपि श्रियम् ॥

*A wife filled with good character, a creeper filled with flowers and speech filled with good meaning attain extraordinary splendour.*

— **Subhashita Manjari - 2.37**

The beauty of a woman is measured by her good character. Thus, the beauty of a chaste wife is incomparable. A creeper is good-looking when it is full of colourful flowers. Speech is beautiful when it is adorned with good meaning. This is when these three attain extraordinary splendour.

199. नरस्याभरणं रूपं रूपस्याभरणं गुणः।
गुणस्याभरणं ज्ञानं ज्ञानस्याभरणं क्षमा ॥

*Beauty is the adornment for a man. Good character is the adornment for beauty. Knowledge is the adornment for good character. Forgiveness is the adornment for knowledge.*

— **Naraabharanam - 2**

Beauty gives man a good look. But beauty devoid of virtue is not valuable. Even the snake looks very beautiful, but no one dares go near it, for it possesses deadly poison. So beauty must be adorned by good character. A proverb says: "Beauty without virtue is like a rose without fragrance." When adorned with knowledge, good character commands respect. And when a person possessing beauty, good character and knowledge also has the quality of forgiveness, he is very great and is indeed the most handsome one.

# Desire

200. आशाया ये दासास्ते दासाः सर्वलोकस्य।
     आशा येषां दासी तेषां दासायते लोकः ॥

*People who are servants of desires are servants to the whole world. For those to whom desire is a servant, the whole world also is a servant.*

—Subhashita Manjari - 8.53

Desire has no end, just as the sky has no end. As we fulfil one desire, another creeps in. A person first likes to ride a bicycle; then he wants to have a scooter, later a car and so on. If one cannot control his desires and becomes a servant to them, he has to be a servant to everyone to fulfil his desires. He has to work to fulfil his desires. On the other hand, if one is a master of desires, he becomes the master of the whole world, for he then does not expect anything from anyone.

The Puranas cite the example of King Yayati, who was cursed by his father-in-law to grow old. He then begged to regain youth, enjoyed objects of heaven and found that all wealth, land and women were not enough for a single man! Thus, one should control his desires to gain peace of mind.

201. आशा नाम मनुष्याणां काचिदाश्चर्यशृंखला।
     यया बद्धाः प्रधावन्ति मुक्तस्तिष्ठति पङ्गुवत् ॥

*Desire is a special chain. Those who are bound in this chain run around and those who are released from this chain stand like lame persons!*

—Nitya Neeti - Pg. 107

People bound in chains, as in prison, cannot move or do anything independently. Once released, they move about in happiness. The poet says that desire is a special chain, when tied to a person, makes him wander about. A person with desires becomes restless, and hankers to have them fulfilled. He cannot stay in one place and remain peaceful. A person who is released from the chain of desires, stands still like a lame person and achieves peace of mind.

202. भोगा न भुक्ता वयमेव भुक्ता
तपो न तप्तं वयमेव तप्ताः।
कालो न यातो वयमेव याताः
तृष्णा न जीर्णा वयमेव जीर्णाः॥

*Pleasures have not been enjoyed. But we ourselves have been devoured. Austerities have not been performed by us, but we ourselves have been scorched. Time never came up to us, but we ourselves went near time. Desires never got reduced, but we ourselves grew old and feeble.*

— Vairagya Shataka - 7

The poet beautifully explains about the endlessness of pleasures and desires by using similar words twice. *Bhuktaah* means both *enjoyed* and *eaten up*. We did not enjoy all pleasures of the world, but we ourselves were eaten up (became old) by time. *Taptaah* (religious austerities) is said to be difficult, like getting up early in the morning, chanting prayers, always being truthful and honest, having self-control etc. We never did all this, but were afflicted by sufferings like disease and difficulties. Good times never came to us. But we approached time (came nearer to our end).

203. वलीभिर्मुखमाक्रान्तं पलितेनाङ्कितं शिरः।
गात्राणि शिथिलायन्ते तृष्णैका तरुणायते॥

*The face has been attacked by wrinkles. The head is tinted white and grey! All the limbs are enfeebled. But desire alone is still youthful and strong.*

— Vairagya Shataka - 8

Sri Shankaracharya has composed a similar verse, which says: "The old man's body has grown feeble, with hairless head and toothless gums. He comes holding a stick, but still hasn't come out of the clutches of desire!" Thus, man grows feeble, but his desires remain strong. Man grows old but suffers to fulfil his desires. One never tries to control them. The result is that one is unable to fulfil all desires and laments and suffers in vain.

204. अपि मेरुसमं प्राज्ञमपि शूरमपि स्थिरम् ।
तृणीकरोति तृष्णैका निमेषेण नरोत्तमम् ॥

*Even though a person is as great as Mount Meru, intelligent, valiant, and steady-minded, desire makes him equal to a blade of grass in a minute!*

— Yogavashishta Vairagya – 17.50

One may be very intelligent, valiant and scholarly like Mount Meru, which is said to be a very great mountain, but even such a person becomes like an insignificant object, like a blade of grass, when he is affected by desire. For fulfilment of desires, people do wrong things and get humiliated.

The Mahabharata gives an example of Vasus, who were eight demi-gods. They were in an exalted position, but they once stole a celestial cow of sage Vasishta, since they were provoked by their wives' desire. Sage Vasishta came to know of this and cursed them that they would be born as human beings. Similarly, sage Vishwamitra was performing a severe penance to acquire virtues that would enable him to become a Bramharshi or an exalted sage. One day, he saw a celestial dancer, Menaka, and was overcome by lust. He forgot his penance in her company and wasted 10 years! Thus, there are many examples of great personalities who disgraced themselves due to desire.

# Anger

205. तिरस्कुर्वन्ति कृतिनस्तापयन्ति तपस्विनः ।
आत्मानमपि हिंसन्ति क्रोधान्धाः किमतः परम् ॥

*People blinded by anger disregard those who have worked for them, hurt holy men and harm themselves. What more can they do?*

— Subhashita Manjari - 8.119

An angry person does not know what he does. His intelligence is overcome by anger and he goes blind. Cato had said: "An angry man opens his mouth and shuts his eyes." People often go to the extent of killing in anger. One forgets that he should respect elders and holy men and blasphemes them in anger. The Puranas give many examples wherein sages curse others in anger without thinking twice. Sage Jamadagni ordered his son Parashurama to kill his own mother, as she kept watching the romance of celestial beings and was thus late for worship. Sage Bhrigu once went to test the greatness of Brahma, Vishnu and Shiva. He first went to Brahma and Shiva and offended them. They were furious and cursed him. Then he visited Vishnu's abode and kicked him in his chest too. But Vishnu smiled and paid him respect. Thus the sage concluded that Vishnu was indeed the greatest, as he had conquered anger.

Lord Rama says: "Prompted by anger, man kills his own mother, father, brother, friends and relations. He will often have occasion to repent actions done under the impulse of anger. Anger destroys one's virtues. So give up anger. Anger is indeed Yama, the great enemy." Therefore, one should control anger.

206. उत्तमे स्यात् क्षणं कोपं मध्यमे घटिकाद्वयम् ।
अधमे स्यादहोरात्रं पापिष्ठे मरणान्तिकम् ॥

*Anger lasts for a second in noble men. It lasts for an hour or two in intermediate or ordinary men. In a mean-minded person it lasts for a whole day and night. In the vilest man it lasts till death!*

— Nitya Neeti - Pg. 3

Even if they get angry, noble people forget it soon and remain as before. Ordinary people may quarrel or not speak for a few hours. A mean-minded person takes the matter seriously and remains angry for the entire day and night. A vile man, however, remains angry and develops life-long hatred. In the story of Romeo and Juliet, we see that both their families had everlasting enmity due to an old incident, because of which the young lovers suffered. Therefore, anger should not be maintained for long. Both parties should forgive and forget.

207. न पूतो न तपस्वी च न यज्वा न च धर्मभाक् ।
क्रोधस्य यो वशं गच्छेत्तस्य लोकद्वयं न हि ॥

*One controlled by anger is not pure, not a holy man, not the one who can perform sacrifices and not righteous. Such a person has no place here or in the other world.*

— Subhashita Manjari - 8.145

Horace said: "Anger is short madness, so control your passion, or it will control you." If one gets angry, it gradually consumes him and leads to unbearable acts. As Pythagoras said: "Anger begins in folly and ends in repentance." The poet says that one, although a holy man, righteous, upright person, shall not be of any good if he cannot control his anger. The story of the Brahmin Koushika supports this.

Kaoshika was a religious Brahmin who performed severe austerities. He had studied the Vedas. One day, while sitting under a tree, a bird let its droppings fall over his head. Enraged, Kaoshika gave the bird a sharp look and the bird was reduced to ash by the fire of his anger! That was the power of his penance, which he wasted in anger. He then went out for alms and a woman was late in getting him food, as she was serving her husband. Kaoshika gave her a sharp look, but nothing happened. Instead, she said: "I am not that poor bird, O Brahmin!" Kaoshika wondered how she knew the incident. She said that since she was very chaste, she knew things, and advised him to give up anger if he wished to progress. She sent him to the hunter, Dharmavyadha, to learn more about righteousness. Thus, because of anger, Kaoshika lost all his greatness.

Anger should be controlled in the very beginning. One needs to condition the mind when he is angry by chanting, just keeping quiet or going out, as anger subsides soon.

208. काम एष क्रोध एष रजोगुणसमुद्भवः।
महाशनो महापाप्मा विद्ध्येनमिह वैरिणम् ॥

*It is desire and anger that have sprung from passion (that make one commit sins). They are voracious eaters, great sinners, and know them to be the enemies of mankind.*

— **Bhagavad Gita - 3.37**

This is a verse spoken by Lord Krishna in answer to a question asked by Arjuna as to why man commits crime though uninterested in it. Lord Krishna says that it is due to desire or lust and anger that follows it. When desire cannot be fulfilled, anger arises, and from anger intelligence is lost. Thus, man commits mistakes and crimes.

209. कुपितोऽपि गुणायैव गुणवान् भवति ध्रुवम्।
स्वभावमधुरं तक्रं मथितं हि रसोत्तमम् ॥

*Noble people do not give up their goodness even if they are angry occasionally, just as curds yield butter even if churned.*

— **Naraabharanam - 30**

Noble people do not get angry and even if angry they do no harm. It is like the anger of parents with an impudent child or of the teacher with a foolish pupil. Their anger is for good.

Kubera's sons were once intoxicated and in the nude with many damsels in a pool. Sage Narada happened to pass by and the damsels covered themselves. But the two impudent sons of Kubera, proud due to their wealth, neither covered themselves nor respected the sage. In order to crush their pride, in anger Narada cursed them to turn into trees! But he also bestowed them with the memory of the Lord. After many years, their forms were restored by Lord Krishna. Thus, from this story we learn that noble people do well even when angry.

# Contentment

210. अकिञ्चनस्य दान्तस्य शान्तस्य समचेतसः ।
सदा सन्तुष्टमनसः सर्वाः सुखमया दिशः ॥

*All places give happiness to one who is self-controlled, peaceful, steady-minded and always contented even though poor.*

— Suktimala - 341

Herein it is stated that one lives happily in any place if he is self-controlled, peaceful and contented. A story goes that a king once wanted to find out the happiest man in his country. He sent his men to find out such a man and his men enquired from all rich men. All the rich people were very unhappy, restless and fearful. They were full of the desire to increase their money, envious of other rich men and worried that someone would snatch their wealth. Finally, the king and his men were informed that there was a cobbler who happened to be the happiest man. The king went to see him and, to his surprise, saw that the man lived in small hut and had only a single pair of clothing. When asked how he was happy, the cobbler explained that he was content with whatever he had earned and was therefore happy. Thus, contentment brings peace of mind and happiness.

211. गोशतादपि गोक्षीरं प्रस्थं ग्रामशतादपि ।
प्रासादादपि खट्वार्धं शेषं परिविभूतये ॥

*One requires the milk of one cow, though he possesses one hundred cows. One needs only a measure of grain though he owns a hundred villages. One needs only half a cot though he has a big palace. The rest belongs to others.*

—**Subhashita Manjari – 14.504**

One may own a hundred cattle, but he requires the milk of one cow only everyday. Likewise, though one owns a hundred villages, he requires only a measure of rice for a day, and half a cot to sleep, though he lives in a big palace.

This implies that the basic necessities of man are minimal. But due to greed and covetousness, fights arise between men. The difference between an animal and man is that an animal is self-satisfied and does not take more than necessary. For example, if there is bag full of rice, a bird alights, eats its fill and flies away, whereas a man takes the whole bag with him. Here, the poet conveys that one should be content with what he has and use his extra possessions for societal good.

# Sacrifice

212. त्यजेदेकं कुलस्यार्थे ग्रामस्यार्थे कुलं त्यजेत् ।
ग्रामं जनपदस्यार्थे आत्मार्थे पृथिवीं त्यजेत् ॥

*One must be sacrificed for the good of a family. A family has to be sacrificed for the welfare of a village. A village has to be sacrificed for the welfare of a country. The whole earth has to be sacrificed for the good of the Self.*

— Hitopadesha - 2.115

This verse says that one must be sacrificed to save the family. When a person in a family is found to be a wicked man harming the family or society, he must be handed over to the law without considering his relationship. This likewise applies to a village and country. In the Mahabharata, the eldest of the Kauravas, Duryodhana was a wicked person. Vidura, the intelligent minister, advised Dhritarashtra, the father of the Kauravas, to drive him out and sacrifice him, so that the remaining 99 brothers could be saved. But the father did not heed his words. The result? Duryodhana cheated his cousins, the Pandavas, and a war broke out, in which all the Kauravas, including respectable elders of the family, died.

A story from the Puranas says that a king called Sagara had a son named Asamanjas. He was so wicked that he drowned small children in the river! For the welfare of society, Sagara drove him out of the country. The verse says that for the good of the Self, one must sacrifice the entire earth. This means that for Self-realisation, one should give up ideas of relations, friends and worldly pleasures, which are temporary. In other words, one must work without attachment.

# Fame

213. चलं चित्तं चलं वित्तं चलं जीवनयौवनम् ।
चलाचलमिदं सर्वं कीर्तिर्यस्य स जीवति ॥

*The mind moves (is fickle-minded), money moves and life and youth move, everything moves (is temporary). One who has fame lives (always).*

— **Nitya Neeti - Pg. 70**

The mind does not remain at one point always. It flits from one subject to another. For example, a baby likes to play with balloons, but a young boy does not like balloons. He may like to play cricket or football. A youth would be interested in a female, while an old man likes religious values. Thus, the mind is never focussed. Money is similar. One may have lots of money and wish to remain rich, but may become poor after some time. A person may be healthy, well built and handsome in his youth, but turns old gradually and loses his strength and beauty.

Thus, everything in this world is temporary, except fame. For long, many will remember a person famous through his noble work. Rabindranath Tagore became famous through his work, *Gitanjali* (a collection of poems for which he was awarded the Nobel Prize). Mother Teresa was known through her service, Gandhiji through his noble values, M.S. Subbulakshmi and Lata Mangeshkar for their excellent singing, etc. Therefore, one should try to earn fame, rather than money and beauty.

214. गच्छन् शरीरविच्छेदावपि भस्मावशेषताम् ।
कर्पूरः सौरभेणैव जन्तुः ख्यात्यानुमीयते ॥

*Even when a person dies and leaves his body, which burns to ashes, he is still remembered for his good deeds, just as camphor exudes good aroma even while it burns. Thus, a man is measured by his fame.*

— Rajatarangini - 7.14.35

Death or an end is common to all living and non-living things on earth. But some like camphor, though they end themselves when burnt, emit a useful and pleasing aroma. Similarly, though noble men die, they continue to live through their noble ideas, books, songs and good deeds. Fame makes one immortal.

215. अन्यमाश्रयते लक्ष्मीस्त्वन्यमन्यं च मेदिनी ।
अनन्यगामिनी पुंसां कीर्तिरेका पतिव्रता ॥

*Lakshmi (wealth) and earth leave one person and go to another. Fame alone stays with one, forever, like a loyal wife.*

— Suktimala - 263

A wife is called *pativrata*, or chaste, when she remains loyal to her husband. Wealth and land (earth) are compared to wives, which belong to a person. But they do not stay with the same person for long. A person who is rich today may become penniless tomorrow. A poor man may likewise become very rich. Money thus moves from person to person. The goddess of money, Lakshmi, is therefore called *Chanchalaa* or fickle-minded. A person who owns land may be conquered by another one day, who then owns the land. After death, the money and the land pass on to another person.

But fame, on the other hand, always remains with one person, both during his life and even after death. No one can own the fame of Rabindranath Tagore even though he is no more. Thus, the poet humorously calls fame *pativrata*.

216. घटं भिन्द्यात् पटं छिन्द्यात् कुर्याद्वा गार्दभस्वनम् ।
येन केन प्रकारेण प्रसिद्धपुरुषो भवेत् ॥

*Fame should be gained somehow, either by breaking a pot or by tearing a cloth or by shouting like an ass!*

— Subhashita Manjari - 14.506

The poet has humorously portrayed how a person who is not famous tries foolishly to gain fame. Fame should be gained by good deeds, or there is no need to become famous. But one should not try to gain fame by foolish methods. There are many people who try to gain fame by getting awards through money and influence.

A story from Kathasaritsagara relates that a Brahmin who had not studied anything wanted to become famous. One day, there was a marriage function at his neighbour's house. He stole the bridegroom's horse in the night and sent his wife the next day to announce that he was a good astrologer and could predict the whereabouts of the horse. As she did so, the whole party came and requested him to predict its whereabouts. As he himself had hid the horse, he predicted its hiding place and they found it! He thus became famous but had problems later on in his life as he was always called for predictions!

# Foresight

217. चिन्तनीया हि विपदामादावेव प्रतिक्रिया।
 न कूपखननं युक्तं प्रदीप्ते वह्निना गृहे ॥

*One should think of remedies for problems before they arise.*
*It is not wise to dig a well when the house is on fire.*

— Suktimala - 301

One should anticipate dangers that might arise in future and think of remedies to solve them. Water is required to extinguish fire when the house is burning. But one cannot dig a well for water when the house is on fire! This has to be done beforehand, anticipating the danger. Thus, the poet cites this example to emphasise the importance of foresight. A famous proverb says: "Forewarned is forearmed."

# Duty

218. अकर्तव्यं न कर्तव्यं प्राणैः कण्ठगतैरपि ।
कर्तव्यमेव कर्तव्यं प्राणैः कण्ठगतैरपि ॥

*That which must not be done should never be done, even if life is about to leave one. Duty alone has to be done even when life is about to ebb.*

—Nitya Neeti - Pg. 18

One should be dutiful even if it costs him his life and one should not do wrong deeds to protect his life. In the Mahabharata, we find that Arjuna wanted to flee from his duty of fighting, since he was faced with the prospect of killing his cousins, elders and other relatives. At that moment, Lord Krishna explained to him about his duties and advised him that it was his duty to fight wicked people although they were his relatives.

One may come across such a situation where a policeman has to arrest his own kith and kin charged with a crime and it is his duty to do this impartially. It was the duty of Lord Rama as a son to obey his father and he did so, even though he had to go into exile in a forest for 14 years. Thus one should do his duty at all costs.

# Precious Jewels

219. धर्मो यशो मयो दाक्ष्यं मनोहारि सुभाषितम् ।
इत्यादि गुणरत्नानां संग्रही नावसीदति ॥

*One who collects righteousness, fame, morality, compassion, mind-pleasing Subhashitas (words of wisdom), and other precious jewels of good virtues never becomes sorrowful.*

—Suktimala - 11

Everyone is fond of collecting different jewels. But these jewels give temporary happiness, and they may even get lost, thereby causing much misery to their owner. The jewels of good qualities are those mentioned by the poet, like righteousness, fame, morality, compassion, and especially *Subhashitas* (words of wisdom) that, once owned, are then never lost. One need not be afraid of anyone robbing these, nor worry about having to hide them. They always remain with the original person and come to his assistance when required. *Subhashitas* of great people direct one onto the right path and help one progress in life. One should therefore collect these wise, immortal sayings from books and people of wisdom.

# Unity

220. अल्पानामपि वस्तूनां संहतिः कार्यसाधिका ।
तृणैर्गुणत्वमापन्नैर्बध्यन्ते मत्तदन्तिनः ॥

*Even weak objects achieve a target when they join together. Even elephants can be tied with a rope made of grass that is lumped together.*

— Hitopadesha - 2.27

When taken individually, grass is very weak. But if lumped together, grass can be turned into a rope with which even a mighty animal like the elephant can be tied up. Another Sanskrit verse cites the example of ants that are individually weak, but when they come together they can devour a serpent. Thus, unity imparts strength, by which even weak people can accomplish great tasks. An Aesop fable illustrates this.

A farmer had four sons who were always quarrelling and never heeded his advice. One day, he gave them a bundle of sticks and asked each of them to break the bundle. None of them could break it. He then separated the bundle and gave them each an individual stick and asked them to break it, which they easily broke. He explained to his sons that if they too remained united like the bundle, no enemy could harm them and they could achieve anything. On the other hand, if they quarrelled and were divided, they could easily be overcome by anyone. This principle applies to our countrymen particularly, for in India we have different cultures, languages and religions. But we should always stay united. This was the teaching of all freedom fighters. A proverb is apt: "United we stand, divided we fall."

# Kings and Rulers

221. राज्ञि धर्मिणि धर्मिष्ठाः पापे पापपराः सदा ।
राजानमनुवर्तन्ते यथा राजा तथा प्रजाः ॥

*If the king is righteous, his people will be righteous. If the king is a sinner, his people will be sinners. People follow the ruler. As the king is, so are the people.*

—Subhashita Manjari - 9.65

The king is said to be a representative of God (राजा प्रत्यक्षदैवता— "King is God who has appeared"). Such a position is ascribed to him because he protects his people from evil and vile men, and enemies from outside the kingdom. He also takes an interest in ascertaining the difficulties of his people and works to relieve them from their problems. He should improve righteousness, and virtues among people, and thus make his kingdom a heaven. An ideal kingdom is compared to Lord Rama's kingdom and is called Ramarajya, since there was no vice or evil during the reign of Lord Rama and people were happy and content.

Therefore, a good king should himself be righteous and abstain from vice. Present-day politicians and leaders are the present kings and they should follow this verse. It is the tendency of people to follow a great man, as stated by the Lord in the *Gita*: यद्यदाचरति श्रेष्ठस्तत्तदेवेतरो जनाः । "As the great people do, so the rest follow." Hence, if the leader is virtuous, people will be virtuous. If the leader himself is vile, people also become like that.

222. लोकरञ्जनमेवात्र राज्ञां धर्मः सनातनः ।
सत्यस्य रक्षणं चैव व्यवहारस्य चार्जवम् ॥

*The eternal duty of kings is to keep their people happy. Also, protection of truth and being honest in affairs and conduct are their duties.*

— Suktimala - 451

*Ranjana* means 'pleasing', or 'to give happiness', and since a king pleases his subjects, he is called raja: राजा प्रकृतिरञ्जनात् । As mentioned earlier, a king or a leader of the community should ascertain the problems of his people and solve them. This pleases them and ensures their happiness. A leader should also collect taxes reasonably from people. He must protect the truth by punishing evil people and preventing evil deeds through strict vigilance. He should himself be righteous. A king of bad conduct will have to face the wrath of the people.

The *Bhagavatam* relates the story of King Vena who, due to his bad conduct, was killed by sages who had come to advise him on behalf of the people. His son Prithu, on the other hand, was an ideal king and from him the earth, which was divided by him into villages and countries, got the name *Prithvi.*

# Master and Servant

223. दाता क्षमी गुणग्राही स्वामी दुःखेन लभ्यते।
शुचिर्दक्षोऽनुरक्तश्च जाने भृत्योऽपि दुर्लभः ॥

*It is difficult to get a master who is generous, one who forgives, and one who appreciates the good qualities in others; and it is also difficult to get a servant who is pure, honest, efficient, contented and loyal.*

—Suktimala - 265

It is a common experience that masters or employers are generally proud due to their high position, are not generous, and do not appreciate the good qualities in their servants. Similarly, servants do the job without interest, and many of them may not be honest. Since many receive a low salary, they become corrupt. Many may not be contented with what they get. It is said: "A bad master makes a bad servant." The poet describes the ideal qualities that a good master and a good servant should have in them, and says that it is very difficult to get such people.

# Women

224. यत्र नार्यस्तु पूज्यन्ते रमन्ते तत्र देवताः।
यत्रैतास्तु न पूज्यन्ते सर्वास्तत्राफला क्रियाः॥

*Gods feel happy at those places where women are respected. All tasks remain unfulfilled where women are disrespected.*

—Manu Smriti - 3.56

A woman is compared to the divine goddess Adi Shakti (the primeval power) who is the power of Trimurti, the three principal gods of creation, maintenance and annihilation, viz, Brahma, Vishnu and Shiva. The greatness of women is glorified in Hindu scriptures. The woman as a daughter serves her parents, as a wife gives love and affection to her husband, and as a mother, she is responsible for the continuity of the race. Therefore, it is said: "Behind every successful man there is a woman." Another proverb says: "The hand that rocks the cradle rules the world."

Women are power. They are skilful, intelligent and the country where they are respected prospers. Manu says that even the Gods become happy where women are respected and tasks remain unfulfilled where they are not. The Mahabharata says women are comparable to Goddess Lakshmi and they should be kept happy through presents of clothes and jewels. If a woman happens to weep, it is said that the family is destroyed. There are many examples in the scriptures to show that people were destroyed when they insulted women. Though a mighty warrior, Ravana was killed by Lord Rama when he abducted Sita. Duryodhana, the chief of the Kauravas, attempted to insult Draupadi by stripping off her clothes, as a result of which he and his brothers were ultimately slain by Bhima. Similarly, Keechaka tried to molest Draupadi and was killed by Bhima.

At another place, Manu says that women should not be given independence and must be protected by a father, husband or son. This is only with respect to protection, as women are by nature weak. But this was misunderstood in the earlier period and men made women their slaves without allowing them even the liberty to study. There existed horrible social evils like sati, which oppressed women. Women were also harassed for dowry, which still exists as a social evil. Thanks to Raja Ram Mohan Roy and other reformers, many of these social evils were controlled or eradicated. Women should be protected, cared and given more opportunities for learning, earning and improving their lot. Women are now prospering in all fields; their progress ensures a country's prosperity.

225. अकृत्यं मन्यते कृत्यं अगम्यं गम्यते सुगम् ।
अभक्ष्यं मन्यते भक्ष्यं स्त्रीवाक्यप्रेरितो नरः ॥

*A man prompted by a woman thinks an evil deed to be a good one, the place where one should not go to be a good place and that which should not be eaten as good to eat.*

— Panchatantra - 2.151

In this verse, we see that women attract men by their charm and spoil them. An example given in the Puranas is of sage Vishwamitra, who was performing a severe penance to become an exalted sage when Indra sent a celestial dancer Menaka to interrupt his penance. Attracted by her charms, he lived with her and wasted 10 years. Men cannot control their lust for women and become slaves of their senses. There are many instances where obedient sons have abandoned parents under pressure from their wives. Hence it is said: "Woman is the salvation or destruction of the family." The *Bhagavatam* says that one who is addicted to women loses his self-respect, knowledge, virtue and fame.

Once a she-goat had fallen into a pit. It happened to see a male goat pass nearby. It attracted the male goat with its charms. The male foolishly jumped into the pit. The she-goat said that it would jump out with the help of the he-goat and then get him out too. The male goat agreed and bowed its head. The she-goat clambered over it and got out of the pit. The poor male goat was stranded in the pit. Thus, men attracted by the charms of women act foolishly.

# Teacher

### 226. गुरवो बहवः सन्ति शिष्यवित्तापहारकाः ।
### दुर्लभः स गुरुर्लोके शिष्यचित्तापहारकाः ॥

*There are many teachers who work with the student's money in mind. The teacher who works with the student's welfare in mind is rare.*

— **Subhashita Manjari - 13.22**

In today's world, teaching has become a commercial enterprise. In the Vedic period, there were Gurukulas – places where both rich and poor students stayed and served their teachers, while learning at the same time. Teachers taught wholeheartedly without any selfish motives. After the period of education was over, students would present the teachers *Guru Dakshina* or the fees for learning. Now, most teachers want money and do not bother about teaching well. In order to revive the system of Gurukulas, Rabindranath Tagore opened Shantiniketan, where students learn amidst peace and harmony.

In the present age of Kaliyuga, there are many so-called spiritual teachers who try to mint money by duping people into performing costly rituals. Many proclaim themselves as reincarnations of God and mislead people. It is rare to come across a real guru, a spiritual teacher who advises the simple, spiritual path of devotion and attracts people's minds towards true knowledge.

227. कुरु गुरुवचो निपीतं
भूयो भूयो विचिन्तयाधीतम् ।
विद्या गुरूपदिष्टा चिर
परिविष्टा विभूषणं वपुषः ॥

*Imbibe the teachings of the guru. Contemplate his teachings over and over. If the knowledge imparted by the teacher is contemplated, it uplifts one's body.*

**— Hari Hara Subhashita - 3.3**

The Upanishads say: आचार्यदेवोभव । – "Revere your teacher as God." The *Bhagavatam* says that the teacher is a representative of God and one must adhere to his teachings and ponder over them regularly. When doubts arise, one must modestly approach the teacher for clarification, as advised by the Lord in the *Gita*: तद्विद्धि प्रणिपातेन परिप्रश्नेन सेवया । – "Learn that knowledge by respectful obeisance, questioning and service." When one gains knowledge in this way, it is akin to a decorative ornament for him.

# Rarities

**228.** जननी जन्मभूमिश्च जाह्नवी च जनार्दनः ।
जनकः पञ्चमश्चैव जकाराः पञ्च दुर्लभाः ॥

*Janani (Mother), Janma Bhumi (the birthplace), Jaahnavi (River Ganga), Janardhana (God), and Janaka (Father) – these five that start from the letter 'Ja' are rarities.*

—Subhashita Ratnavali - 16.350

It is said: "Mother is the name for God on the lips and in the hearts of little children." A mother takes the sacred place of God, since she undergoes lot of pain to bring one on earth, and then bestows the utmost care and love on the child to ensure it doesn't suffer the slightest discomfort. The birthplace is said to be another mother for us, as it provides us food, water, air and shelter. We always owe a debt to our birthplace. The Ganga River is said to be the most sacred river, since it emanated from the lotus feet of Lord Vishnu. It washes away the sins of those who bathe in it. Devotion to God is the greatest act, which bestows peace, happiness and contentment. A father provides education, teaches moral values to a child and feels most happy when his child makes his mark. Thus, these five are rarities.

**229.** दानं प्रियवाक्सहितं ज्ञानमगर्वं क्षमान्वितम् ।
वित्तं त्यागनियुक्तं दुर्लभं एतच्चतुर्भद्रम् ॥

*Charity done with pleasing words, knowledge devoid of pride, valour associated with forgiveness, wealth associated with sacrifice – these four noble qualities are found very rarely.*

—Hitopadesha - 2.122

Generally, people who give charity become proud and speak arrogantly. So, it is rare to find one who gives charity, but remains humble and talks pleasantly. A warrior is always interested in vanquishing his enemy and it is rare to find one who, though powerful and brave, forgives the enemy. This quality of forgiveness makes even an enemy a friend. When one is learned, he becomes proud. It is rare to find a wealthy person who uses his money for service and is ready to sacrifice and help those in need. Thus, people with such qualities are rare.

# Always Wonderful

230. गान्धर्वं गन्धसंयुक्तं ताम्बूलं भारती तथा।
इष्टा भार्या प्रियं मित्रमपूर्वाणि दिने दिने ॥

*The Gandharva arts, namely music and dance, good flavoured areca nuts with betel leaves, good poetic work, a devoted wife and a good friend appear wonderful everyday.*

—Suktimala - 212

Music is an art that pleases one, whenever he hears it. Though music may be heard and dance witnessed everyday, they still appear new and refreshing. These two are termed the arts of the Gandharvas, who are celestial beings. Similarly, flavoured betel leaves and areca nuts are enjoyed after meals, and though consumed many times before, they are always pleasing. A good, loving wife is a source of happiness. And a good poetic work is read repeatedly with pleasure. Similarly, talking to a good friend, though done regularly, gives happiness.

# Elevation and Downfall

231. उद्धरेदात्मनात्मानं नात्मानमवसादयेत् ।
आत्मैव ह्यात्मनो बन्धुरात्मैव रिपुरात्मनः ॥

*One should rise by one's own efforts. One should not degrade oneself. One can be a friend to oneself or one's own enemy.*

— Bhagavad Gita - 6.5

It is often said: "Our future is in our hands." Each person is potentially strong and can rise in his own way. Similarly, one can also cause one's own downfall. Lord Krishna says that we ourselves are responsible for our elevation or downfall. We have to depend on teachers and books initially for our knowledge and uplift, but ultimately we progress by our own sincere efforts. It is well said that a horse can be taken to the water, but it cannot be made to drink.

One must also not degrade oneself. Ramakrishna Paramahansa gives an example. A king once insisted that a monk should help him get rid of worldly illusions. The monk grabbed a pillar and shouted that he wanted to be released! The king tried in vain, failed and then told the monk that it was he himself who was holding on to the pillar. Likewise, said the monk, it was the king himself who was living in illusion and he had to come out of it himself. Thus, we nourish fears and negative ideas ourselves and cause our own downfall. Therefore, we must ourselves strive for progress.

232. आरोप्यते शिला शैले यथा यत्नेन भूयसा।
निपात्यते सुखेनाधस्तथात्मा गुणदोषयोः ॥

*A rock is hauled to the top of a hill with great difficulty. But it is easily pushed down. Similarly, one rises with good qualities, but easily falls due to a single misdeed.*

— Hitopadesha - 1.41

One has to put intense efforts to haul a rock to the top of the hill. Similarly, one has to work hard to acquire a good position and reputation. But just as the rock can be easily pushed down with a single shove, likewise a person can earn disrepute with a single misdeed. The Mahabharata cites the example of Nahusha, a king, who was chosen by the gods to become the Lord of Heaven, as they were pleased by his virtues. He thus rose to a very exalted level. Thereafter, he became proud and arrogant and once ordered the seven great sages to carry him in a palanquin. They did so, but since sage Agastya was short, he could not keep pace with the others. Enraged, King Nahusha kicked Agastya! The sage was livid and cursed Nahusha that he would become a serpent. Thus, Nahusha engineered his own downfall. Therefore, once we achieve a good reputation, we should try to maintain it without committing any mistakes.

233. अधोऽधः पश्यतः कस्य महिमा नोपचीयते।
उपर्युपरि पश्यन्तः सर्व एव दरिद्रति ॥

*Whose position does not appear high when one looks at a person lower than him? As one sees a person higher up, everyone else seems to be situated low.*

— Hitopadesha - 1.2

This verse teaches us that a high or low position is only relative, and we should be contented and happy when we see people in lower positions. A person who has a two-wheeler should not be envious of one who moves in a car, but feel happy that he is better than one with a bicycle. One with a bicycle is higher than one who walks. One who walks is better off than one without legs.

There was once a stonecutter who, on seeing a rich man, felt he should become a rich man. A fairy fulfilled his wish. One day he realised that a high-ranking official was greater than the rich, and he wanted to be one. So, he became one. Then one day he went to a hillside and, as it was a very hot day, he felt the sun was greater and wished he was the sun! By the fairy's grace, he became the sun and felt happy. But one day, he was covered by a thick black cloud and wishing to become one, he turned into a cloud. A strong wind, however, dispersed him into many pieces. He next became the wind and blew harder. But he was stopped by a hill and next became a hill. The next day, a group of stonemasons came and began cutting the hill. He then became the original stonecutter he was and found happiness in his own work!

# Death

234. पण्डिते चैव मूर्खे च बलवत्यपि दुर्बले ।
ईश्वरे च दरिद्रे च मृत्योः सर्वत्र तुल्यता ॥

*A scholar, a fool, the strong, weak, wealthy, and poor – all are equal in death.*

—Subhashita Manjari - 12.93

In the Mahabharata, there is a sequence called the Yaksha Prashna or questions by the yaksha. In this, a yaksha asks Yudhishthira many questions, which he answers perfectly. One of the questions is: what is the strangest thing in the world. Yudhishthira answers that though people see someone or the other dying daily, yet they think they will live forever – this is the strangest thing in the world. Each one of us lives in pride, designating ourselves as scholars, intelligent, wealthy, poor, foolish etc. But death sees everyone equally. None can escape death. Hence it is said: "Death is a great leveller."

235. इदं कृतमिद कार्यमिदमन्यत् कृताकृतम् ।
एवमीहासमायुक्तं कृतान्तः कुरुते वशम् ॥

*Death takes one into its custody, who is filled with desires and thinks thus: "I have finished this task. This task is yet to be done. Another task has been done a little. Little more has to be done."*

—Subhashita Manjari - 7.21

Death or time does not wait for one to complete his tasks. It is always uncertain and merciless. There is no particular age or period for death. One cannot ask death to wait until one has completed the wedding of his son or daughter or seen his grandchildren playing before him. One has to accept death whenever it comes. It is said: "Death has no calendar!"

The Puranas narrate how even mighty men have to die, through the stories of demons. The demons would propitiate Lord Brahma to secure a boon that would make them immortal and Brahma would allow them to choose the form of death they wouldn't suffer. Hiranyakashyapu obtained a benediction that he would not be killed by man, god or animal, and Lord Vishnu came as a half-man, half-lion called Narasimha and killed him! Similarly, Ravana prayed that he should not be killed by a list of beings, but neglected humans. Vishnu incarnated as Rama, a human, and killed him. Thus, death is common to all. It is therefore said: "Every door may be shut but not death's door."

236. मरणं प्रकृतिः शरीरिणां विकृतिर्जीवितमुच्यते बुधैः ।
क्षणम् प्यवतिष्ठते श्वसन् यदि जन्तुर्ननु लाभवानसौ ॥

*Death is natural for embodied ones. Life is accidental, so say the intelligent. Therefore, one should be fortunate to live even for a second.*

— Raghuvansha - 8.87

Everyone generally thinks that death is accidental and ponders over why a person died. But here it is said that life is accidental and death is natural. It means that the body, a product of nature, is made up of five elements of nature, earth, water, fire, air, and ether, and it returns to nature, which is natural. The association of the spark of life with these elements creates living entities, and it is one's fortune to be a living being. So, everyone should try to protect life by taking food and water to maintain good health. If one gives these up, he approaches death, which is natural. Thus, one should enjoy life and work wonders. Rabindranath Tagore said: "Death's stamp gives value to the coin of life, making it possible to buy with life what is truly precious."

# Questions and Answers

The following special verses raise relevant questions and provide apt answers.

237. को धर्मो भूतदया किं सौख्यमरोगिता जगति जन्तोः ।
कः स्नेहः सद्भावः किं पाण्डित्यं परिच्छेदः ॥

*What is righteousness? Compassion to all living beings. What is happiness? People having no disease in the world. What is friendship? Good nature. What is knowledge? To analyse with intelligence.*

— Hitopadesha - 2.114

To understand that every living being is equal and to display compassion towards all living beings is indeed righteousness. According to a Jataka tale, a king fond of deer meat would go hunting and kill many deer. The deer pleaded that they would present themselves one by one everyday for slaughter and he should not mercilessly kill many deer. The deer were in two groups and each had a king deer. The request was made by the king deer and the king agreed.

One day it was the turn of a pregnant deer and it requested its king to arrange another deer so that its young one could be saved. The king deer disagreed. The poor pregnant deer requested the king of the other group, and that king, in order to save this deer, itself went to the venue of slaughter! The king came to know of this from his butcher and enquired from the king deer the reason for its act. When he heard the story, he realised the pains of violence and death, and gave up eating deer meat. Then, at the deer's request, he gave up eating the meat of all animals. Thus, compassion is the greatest Dharma.

Similarly, to enjoy health is the greatest happiness, since "health is wealth". Friendship does not mean to give good gifts or enjoy one's company. Good nature, which involves helping each other, is true friendship. Knowledge is not merely studying and remembering big words, but analysing a situation and solving it with intelligence.

238. कोऽन्धो योऽकार्यरतः
को बधिरो यो हितानि न श्रुणोति ।
को मूको यः काले
प्रियाणि वक्तुं न जानाति ॥

*Who is a blind man? He who does wrong deeds. Who is a deaf man? He who does not listen to good words. Who is a dumb man? He who does not know how to speak pleasingly when needed.*

— **Prashnottara Ratna Maalika – 21**

The poet explains who are handicapped in the real sense. We often pity people who are blind, deaf, lame or dumb, but we forget that though we are bestowed with precious gifts like sight, speech etc, we do not make full use of them. Saint Purandaradasa said: "Human life is great. Do not waste it, oh fools!"

Thus, we should use our sight to see and do good deeds, and not indulge in wrong deeds, knowing them to be wrong. It is like a man who falls into a pit despite knowing it's a pit! Similarly, we should use our ears to hear good words and our tongue to speak pleasingly.

239. किं मरणं मूर्खत्वं
किं चानर्घं यदवसरे दत्तम् ।
आमरणात् किं शल्यं
प्रच्छन्नं यत्कृतं पापम् ॥

*What is death? Foolishness! What is most precious? That given at the proper time to the proper person. What is it that torments one till death? Sins committed in secrecy.*

— **Prashnottara Ratna Maalika – 14**

A proverb says, "Fools die young and look sick." Foolishness is almost like death, for a fool not only fails to accomplish a task, but also gets humiliated everywhere. Therefore, one should befriend the wise, read good books and become wise and intelligent. A thing given to the right person at the time of necessity is more precious than the most precious jewel. The guilt of a sin committed in secrecy torments one till death, for his conscience knows it to be wrong.

An anecdote of the great saint Kanakadasa is relevant. Kanakadasa's teacher once gave him and his other disciples a banana each and asked them to eat it where no one would see them eating. Accordingly, everyone ate the fruit in different hiding places, except Kanakadasa. When the teacher questioned him, Kanakadasa replied, "God is everywhere and he definitely sees me eating." The teacher was happy with him. Thus, sin cannot be performed in secrecy.

240. किं मित्रमन्ते सुकृतं न लोकाः
किं ध्येयमीशस्य पदं न शोकाः।
किं काम्यमव्याजसुखं न भोगाः
किं जल्पनीयं हरिनाम नान्यत् ॥

*Who is a friend at the end of one's life? The merit of good deeds, not people. What should be thought about? God's lotus feet, not worries. What should one desire? Eternal happiness, not worldly pleasures. What should be uttered? The Lord's name and nothing else.*

— **Subhashita Manjari - 13.19**

At the time of death, when a person has to leave the body, no friend or relative goes along with him. He has to reach heaven or hell, or take birth again in a noble or poor family, depending upon his past actions. If one does good deeds during his lifetime, the merits of those deeds follow him and ensure a good destiny. Worries, if pondered upon, burn one's mind and torment him. Therefore, one should think of the lotus feet of God, so that solutions can be found for problems. Worldly pleasures are always tainted with sorrow.

Hence, one must give up greed and live contentedly, which ensures happiness. People utter all kinds of uncivilised words and quarrel. Instead, one should chant the Lord's holy names, which purify one's mind, and ensure happiness.

Sri Shankaracharya says: भज गोविन्दं गोविन्दं भज मूढमते । "O fool! Chant the name of Govinda, chant the name of Govinda, and chant the name of Govinda! Knowledge of grammar won't help you at the time of death." Thus, one must chant God's name for deliverance from miseries.

241. साधुबलं किं दैवं कः साधुः सर्वदा तुष्टः ।
दैवं किं यत्सुकृतं कः सुकृती श्लाघ्यते च यः सद्भिः ॥

*What is power for the noble man? God. Who is a noble man? One who is always satisfied. What is God? Merit of good deeds. What is good deed? That which is apprised by virtuous people.*

—Prashnottara Ratna Maalika - 48

The poet raises questions and answers them intelligently. A noble man indeed acquires strength from God, Who is in the form of good deeds. A noble man is he who is ever satisfied, one who does not have greed and covetousness. Good deeds are those that include serving the poor, planting trees, building hospitals and temples, reading the scriptures etc.

242. किं दुःखमसन्तोषः किं जाड्यं पाठतोऽप्यनभ्यासः ।
किं गुरुताया मूलं यदेतदप्रार्थनं नाम ॥

*What is sorrow? Not to be contented. What is laziness? Not to practise what one has studied. What is respect? Not to beg before others.*

—Nithya Neeti - Pg. 105

One who is not content with whatever he earns or has, and hankers after something, becomes restless. Such a person can never be happy. So happiness comes from being contented. One who just studies but never applies that knowledge in life is said to be lazy and he eventually forgets what he has studied. Therefore, it is said: "Practise what you preach." One who earns his livelihood by any rightful means is a respectable man. A person who begs, however, loses respect.

243. का दुर्लभा मनुष्याणां हरिभक्तिः
पातकं च किं हिंसा।
को हि भगवत् प्रियः स्यात्
योऽन्यं नोद्विजयेदनुद्विग्नः ॥

*What is rare to humans? Devotion to the Lord. What is sin? Violence. Who is dear to God? He who never gets agitated by others or never agitates others.*

— Prashnottara Ratna Maalika - 42

Devotion to God is the rarest virtue found in human beings. Many people pray to God for fulfilment of various desires, but a true devotee loves God without praying for anything. The Lord Himself says in the *Gita*: "It is after many births that a man with knowledge surrenders to Me." (बहूनां जन्मानामन्ते ज्ञानवान् मां प्रपद्यते ।)". There are many sins, like lying, robbery etc, but no sin is equal to the violence that harms anyone or any animal, physically or mentally. One must understand that every living being loves to live and so, should not kill or harm any living being. A devotee of God serves everyone and does not disturb or agitate anyone. Similarly, if anyone disturbs him, he does not get agitated and remains calm. The Lord says in the *Gita* (12.15) that one who never agitates anyone and never gets agitated by anyone and one who is free from excitement, fear and anxiety is dear to Him.

# Poison

244. वृश्चिकस्य विषं पुच्छं मक्षिकस्य विषं पदम् ।
 तक्षकस्य विषं दन्तं सर्वाङ्गं दुर्जने विषम् ॥

*In case of a scorpion, the tail is poisonous. In case of a fly, the poison is in its legs. In case of a snake, the poison is in its fangs. In a wicked person, however, the whole body is poisonous.*

— Nitya Neeti - Pg. 68

The poet ironically says that the whole body of a wicked man is poisonous, compared to a scorpion, which has poison in its tail, a fly, which has poison in its legs, in the form of germs, and a snake, which has poison only in its fangs. We already know that these creatures are poisonous and also know how they transmit the poison to us. By knowing this, we can always avoid danger from them. If a snake's fangs are removed, even the most poisonous snake becomes harmless. But none knows how a wicked man strikes, and it is not easy to avoid his poison. Therefore, the poet claims that a wicked man is the most poisonous and his entire body is filled with poison.

245. निर्धनस्य विषं भोगो निस्सत्वस्य विषं रणम् ।
 अनभ्यासो विषं शास्त्रं अजीर्णे भोजनं विषम् ॥

*Pleasure forms poison for a poor man. War is poison for a coward. Scriptures and knowledge are poison for one who never studies and practises. Food is poison for one who cannot digest it.*

— Nitya Neeti - Pg. 11

It is said that one man's food is another man's poison. Thus, for a poor man, wealth appears poisonous, for he cannot enjoy it. For a coward, going to war brings discomfort and appears like poison, as he is afraid of fighting. For one who is lazy, knowledge is poison, as he does not like to study. Similarly, one who has a severe stomach ailment and cannot digest food avoids it. Though all these are good, they appear harmful in different circumstances.

Aesop's fable of the fox and the grapes illustrates this. A fox tried repeatedly to jump up and get at some grapes, which were out of his reach. Having failed after repeated attempts, he walked away muttering that the grapes were sour. Thus, one who fails to achieve an objective or secure something finds faults in the object. But this is not the right attitude. Instead, one must try to identify his mistakes and analyse whether the target is achievable or not and then act accordingly.

# Penance and Renouncement

246. अहिंसा सत्यवचनमानृशंस्यं दमो घृणा।
एतत्तपो विदुर्धीरा न शरीरस्य शोषणम् ॥

*According to the wise, penance constitutes non-violence, truthfulness, generosity, control of the senses and compassion, but not punishment of the body.*

– Subhashita Samputa – Pg. 20

*Tapas* or penance is generally thought to be punishment for the body, like fasting, meditating while standing on one leg, or sitting in between posts of fire, or standing in a river etc. Here, it is stated that real penance is inculcating qualities like non-violence, truthfulness, compassion, control of the senses, generosity etc. Anyone can develop these qualities and one need not go to the forest and punish himself to perform penance.

On the other hand, there is no use in performing severe penance without these qualities. The demons, for example, performed penance for many years to obtain boons from Lord Brahma, but then became too wicked. Lord Krishna says in the *Gita* that the power to enjoy worldly pleasures is reduced by fasting and abstaining, but the desire for them is not reduced. The remedy to overcome desire is through work, surrendering the fruits of action to the God and by detachment. This is called karma yoga. By this, one can develop discipline in one's work and inculcate the above qualities.

247. कामक्रोधावनिर्जित्य किमरण्ये करिष्यति ।
अथवा निर्जितावेतौ किमरण्ये करिष्यति ॥

*What can one who cannot control lust and anger do in a forest? Or, what does one do in a forest after he has controlled this?*

—Subhashita Manjari - 8.73

Earlier, people renounced the world and went into the forest to meditate and realise God. Today, many ashrams serve this purpose. But it is to no avail if a person goes into the forest or enters an ashram but has no control over lust, anger, infatuation, jealousy and other negative qualities. Similarly, a person who has controlled this can still stay in the world, amidst people, and try to realise God.

The *Bhagavatam* cites the example of sage Soubhari. This sage felt that pleasures would attract him even in a forest, so he entered a river to meditate. By his yogic power, he could live underwater also. But there also, he was overcome by lust when he saw the courtship between two fish. He returned to land and got married! After many years, he realised his mistake and returned to meditation. Thus, renunciation involves renunciation of lust, anger, greed etc, and not necessarily of the world.

248. लोभमूलानि पापानि व्याधयो रसमूलकाः ।
स्नेहमूलानि दुःखानि त्रीणि त्यक्त्वा सुखी भवेत् ॥

*Greed is the cause of all sins. Taste is the cause of all disease. Affection is the cause of all sorrow. Therefore, one must renounce these three and live happily.*

—Abhinava Paathaavalli - 1

Desire and greed are the root causes of all sins. To fulfil his desire, man commits sins. One should therefore give up desire and greed, and live contented. Taste implies too much of eating. A person with too much taste eats voraciously, which leads to obesity, diabetes, hypertension, cardiac problems and many other diseases. Hence it is said: "Eat to live but do not live to eat." One should control his appetite and eat limited food. And too much attachment to a person results in excessive sorrow when one loses that person. This implies attachment not just to a person, but also to material objects. So one should not develop too much interest in any object, as it causes sorrow when the object of one's affection or desire is lost. Therefore, one must control desire, taste and attachment to be happy.

249. इन्द्रियाणां विचरतां विषयेष्वपहारिषु ।
संयमे यत्नमातिष्ठेद्विद्वान् यन्तेव वाजिनाम् ॥

*A wise person should control his senses, which get involved in attractive worldly pleasures, just as a charioteer controls the horses.*

— Manu Smriti - 2.88

In the Katha Upanishad, there is a similar passage, where the soul is compared to a passenger in a chariot, which is the body. The living person is the soul and not the body. The horse of this chariot is one's senses and the reins are the mind. Intellect is the charioteer. If the horses gallop in different directions, the chariot is never under control and it may break up. The horses are always moving towards worldly pleasures. If one controls his mind and intellect, he can regulate the movement of the horses (the senses) and then the chariot (the body) moves forward in the right direction. The Vedic scriptures and many great saints like Shankaracharya, Madhava, Chaitanya, Meerabai etc have suggested devotion to God as the best and easiest way to control one's senses. In devotion, one engages his senses in the service of the Lord and thus regulates them. The Lord has also declared devotion to be the best method. Knowledge, which involves self-realisation, should accompany devotion and renunciation but becoming a monk is not easy and not suitable in this age. Instead, one should renounce all vices and excess pleasures, and work with detachment.

# God and the Soul

250. सौवर्णानि सरोजानि निर्मातुं सन्ति शिल्पिनः ।
    तत्र सौरभनिर्माणे चतुरश्चतुराननः ॥

*There are many skilled artisans who can make golden lotuses. But only the four-headed god can create fragrance in them!*

— Subhashita Ratna Samucchaya - 1.6

Man is a wonderful being. He has created wonderful objects, from bullock carts to airplanes, from small toys to computers and robots, and from microscopes to laparoscopes etc. Though man has created many wonderful things, it has not been possible for him to create fragrance in flowers. Man has created a computer with 'brains', but it works only when operated by a living force, the man himself, and this human brain is God's creation! In the *Bhagavad Gita*, the Lord says, "Whatever is there in this world, that is opulent and splendorous, know all that to have sprung from a portion of My glory."

251. येन केन प्रकारेण यस्य कस्यापि देहिनः ।
    संतोषं जनयेत् प्राज्ञस्तदेवेश्वरपूजनम् ॥

*A wise person should try by any means to please and give happiness to any living entity. This itself is worship of God.*

— Subhashita Manjari - 14.351

A wise man sees every living being as part and parcel of God, and serves every living entity equally. The Lord says in the *Bhagavad Gita*, "One who sees God in every living being and every living being in God is the best of yogis. For him I am not lost, and for Me he is not lost." (6.29, 30). In the same scripture, He also says that one who is wise looks at a learned man, a cow, elephant, dog and a dog-eater in the same manner. Jesus also stressed that one should love everyone as his sisters and brothers, and said that serving people meant serving God.

The great saint-devotee Kanakadasa was once eating his meals. A dog came and picked up a *chapatti*, but when he looked at it, the dog ran away in fear. But Kanakadasa followed the dog and fed it with *chapattis*! Likewise, in the Upanishads, there is another example. Two Brahmins sat for a meal and offered it first to God. Just then a monk who was very hungry came and asked for some food. Both of them refused. The monk then challenged them: "You have offered the food to God. Since God is in me, and I am a part of Him, refusal of food to me is refusal to Him too." The Brahmins agreed and shared their food with him. Thus, we should love and please all living entities.

252. न देवो विद्यते काष्ठे न पाषाणे न मृण्मये।
भावेषु विद्यते देवस्तस्माद्भावो हि कारणम् ॥

*God is not present in wood, or stone, or an idol made of clay. God is present in devotion. Therefore, devotion is very important.*

— Suktimala - 289

In *Srimad Bhagavatam*, sage Kapila (an incarnation of Lord Vishnu) says that those who worship God only in images, but do not recognise Him as the innermost soul of every living being, are like those performing a "ritual in ashes". Thus, one who has devotion recognises God to be present everywhere and in everyone, including in images. A devotee perceives the presence of God in images through devotion. One who has no devotion sees only wood or stone. A king who did not like idol worship once met Swami Vivekananda. To impress upon him the idea behind idol worship, Vivekananda asked the king to spit on his mother's painting. The king was taken aback. Vivekananda then explained that just as he felt devotion for his mother's painting, a devotee too, by virtue of his devotion, perceives God in the image. Idol worship is therefore good to conceive God in the mind, but God must not be restricted only to idols and images. One must learn to see God everywhere.

253. वासांसि जीर्णानि यथा विहाय
नवानि गृह्णाति नरोऽपराणि ।
तथा शरीराणि विहाय जीर्णान्यन्यानि
संयाति नवानि देही ॥

*As one gives up an old garment and wears a new one, the soul gives up the old body and enters a new one.*

— Bhagavad Gita - 2.22

In the war of Kurukshetra between the Pandavas and the Kauravas, Arjuna was overcome by sorrow as he had to kill his own kinsmen. At that time Lord Krishna, who was his charioteer, told him that no one actually dies, or takes birth, but it is the soul that departs from an old body and enters a new one, just as we discard our old clothes and wear new ones. Similarly, the body is a garment for the soul, and the soul gets different kinds of clothes (bodies) like that of a human, animal, bird, or insect, according to its past actions. Krishna revealed that weapons, fire, water or wind could not destroy the soul (2.23). When the body is no more useful to the *prana*, it quits and enters a new body. Thus, one need not lament death, for the person never dies, as he is not the body itself.

Further, in the *Gita*, Sri Krishna says that the soul is a part of Him only and being covered by illusion, it suffers and enjoys in the material world, with the mind and senses (15.7). One can come out of this illusion through karma yoga (action without attachment), jnana yoga (knowledge), and bhakti yoga (devotion). He also speaks about Himself, saying that He is the Supreme God, who descends on earth when righteousness is overruled by evil. He tells Arjuna to fight, as it is his duty to eliminate evil. Thus, by reading the *Bhagavad Gita*, one can learn about the soul, God, and the methods of reunion of the soul with God.

254. आकाशात् पतितं तोयं यथा गच्छति सागरम् ।
सर्वदेवनमस्कारः केशवं प्रतिगच्छति ॥

*As water that falls from the sky (when it rains) flows into the sea, so does the worship of all Gods reach Keshava, or Lord Krishna.*

— Subhashita Ratnavali - 9.180

When it rains, water falls to earth and enters different rivers, at different places. But ultimately, all the rivers join the sea. Similarly, the poet says, worship of different Gods reaches only one God. There are different religions all over the world, and people worship God in different forms and names. Yet ultimately, there is only one God, who manifests Himself in different forms. He is with form and formless, just like the sun and its rays. Thus, Allah, Yehovah, Krishna, Buddha, Shiva, all refer to one God.

In the Vedas, it is stated: एकं सद्विप्रा बहुधा वदन्ति । "The wise call one Truth by different names." In the *Gita*, the Lord says, "He approaches the devotee as the way he prays to Him." (ये यथा मां प्रपद्यन्ते तांस्तथैव भजाम्यहम् । In the *Bhagavatam*, Lord Krishna says that one may be able to count all the stones on earth, but one cannot count His innumerable forms and names. Therefore, people should stop fighting with each other in the name of religion, and live in harmony and peace.

# Devotion

255. विपदो नैव विपदः संपदो नैव संपदः ।
विपद्विस्मरणं विष्णोः संपन्नारायणस्मृतिः ॥

*Calamities are really not calamities. Fortunes are not really fortunes. To forget Lord Vishnu is really the calamity, and to remember Him is fortune.*

— Subhashita Manjari – 13.88

Whenever we face calamities, we are worried, and whenever we are blessed with fortunes, we become happy. But the poet says that these are really neither calamities nor fortunes at all, for one can get out of calamities or lose the fortune in due course. The real calamity, however, is to forget God, our supreme saviour. When we forget Him, we commit sins easily, without having fear of a controller. We also take our life and this world as our permanent abode, and thus take happiness and sorrow seriously. But changes in the world do not affect a devotee, as he is aware that the whole world works as per the Lord's will. He remembers God always and enjoys it.

In the *Bhagavatam* (1.8.25) Queen Kunti, the mother of the Pandavas, prays to Lord Krishna that calamities should occur, so that one remembers the Lord at least then, by which one is liberated.

256. अत्यन्तदुष्टस्य कलेरयमेको महान् गुणः ।
कीर्तनादेव कृष्णस्य मुक्तबन्धः परं व्रजेत् ॥

*In the most vicious age of Kaliyuga, there is only one great quality. One gets released from bondage and attains the Supreme just by chanting the names and glories of Lord Krishna.*

— Vishnu Purana - 6.2.40

Of all the four ages, Kaliyuga is the most vicious. Here, people are evil-minded, have short lifespans, and are afflicted by various diseases and many other problems. Therefore, all the scriptures have prescribed the simplest methods of chanting divine names and the glories of God, which wash away all sins of a person.

The *Bhagavatam* relates the story of Ajamila, who associated with a prostitute and begot ten sons through her. The tenth son was named Narayana, which is also the name of God. Ajamila committed various crimes, like robbery, gambling, drinking alcohol, etc, for the sake of the prostitute. He also abandoned his old parents and chaste wife. When his death arrived, Yamadutas, the servants of Yama (the Lord of death) came to pull him out of his body. Frightened by their fierce looks, he called upon his beloved son Narayana, who was playing nearby. Immediately, four Vishnudutas, servants of Lord Vishnu, came and stopped the Yamadutas. They said that since Ajamila had chanted the Lord's name, though unknowingly, he was freed of all sins. They took him to Vaikuntha – the divine abode of Vishnu.

Thus, the scriptures say, when one chants the divine name, knowingly or unknowingly, he is freed of sins. This does not mean that one can commit sins and then take to chanting. If one does so, that itself becomes a sin. Many great devotees like Purandaradasa, Tukaram, Kabir, Mirabai, Chaitanya and others spread the greatness of chanting, which is the sweetest and the easiest method of worshipping God.

257. पत्रं पुष्पं फलं तोयं यो मे भक्त्या प्रयच्छति ।
    तदहं भक्त्युपहृतमश्नामि प्रयतात्मनः ॥

*I accept a leaf, flower, fruit and water, which are offered to Me by one with love and devotion.*

— Bhagavad Gita - 9.26

Bhakti or devotion requires love and not pomp and show. One need not be rich to please God. The Lord says that He accepts an offering even if one offers a small leaf, a fruit, a flower and a little water with devotion. Therefore, one need not be a very learned man, a great scholar, or a generous man to please God. One should have untainted love and affection. Sudama offered Krishna just parched rice and He was happy. In the Ramayana, Shabari offered a few partly eaten fruits and Rama was satisfied.

Once a fruit vendor came near Krishna's house and the child Krishna brought a handful of rice in His small hands to exchange with the fruits. But by the time He came near the vendor, the rice had fallen from His hands. However, out of love for the child, the fruit vendor gave Him the fruits. When the child went away, she was wonderstruck on seeing her basket full of jewels! Thus, one gains a lot through devotion. As described by the Lord Himself, devotion is very simple. But many people engage in senseless practices like the slaughter of animals, the performance of costly rituals etc, which are meaningless.

# Words of Wisdom

258. मातासमं नास्ति शरीरपोषणं
विद्यासमं नास्ति शरीरभूषणम् ।
पूजासमं नास्ति शरीरतोषणम्
चिन्तासमं नास्ति शरीरशोषणम् ॥

*There is no nourishment to the body equal to the nourishment given by the mother. There is no adornment of the body equal to the adornment of knowledge. There is no peace except that attained by the worship of God. There is no torture to the body equal to the torture given by worries.*

— Subhashita Ratnavali - 11.279

The mother loves her child the most and protects and nourishes it through every possible way. One may eat at a hundred places, but never gets the satisfaction acquired after eating the food offered by one's mother. Various ornaments and gorgeous dresses may decorate the body, but it does not shine if one is devoid of knowledge. One may engage in various activities, like charity, yoga etc for peace of mind, but one gets peace of mind only when he offers a simple prayer to God. Diseases and wounds torture the body, but nothing is equal to the torture of worries that punish one from within. A Sanskrit verse says that worries are similar to the pyre. The difference is that the pyre burns the dead, while worries burn the living.

259. मातृवत् परदारांश्च परद्रव्याणि लोष्टवत् ।
आत्मवत् सर्वभूतानि यः पश्यति स पश्यति ॥

*One who sees the wives of others as his mother, the wealth of others as clay, and all living entities as his own self, really sees.*

—Subhashita Manjari – 14.314

One should not be attracted by the charms and beauty of women who are the wives of others, as this destroys a person. The examples of Ravana, Keechaka, Duryodhana and others have been described. Therefore, this verse says that these women should be looked upon and respected like one's mother. Similarly, if one desires the property of others, then fights, robbery, killing and other sinful activities arise, which destroy the peace of oneself and society.

The best example is Duryodhana. He was rich enough, but he desired to have the wealth of his cousins, the Pandavas. Therefore, he lured them into a game of dice, cheated and insulted them, then forced them into exile in the forest, which culminated in the war in which he was killed. So, one must look down upon others' wealth as if it is useless. When one looks at all living entities as himself, there is no question of violence. One can then understand that if anyone is hurt, he feels the same pain as they do and he does not hurt anyone. Thus, if one follows this verse and lives accordingly, all vices can be prevented.

260. विषादप्यमृतं ग्राह्यं बालादपि सुभाषितम् ।
अमित्रादपि सद्वृत्तममेध्यादपि काञ्चनम् ॥

*One can take nectar even when it is amidst poison. One can hear good words even when spoken by a young one. One may learn about good character even from an enemy. One may take gold even from filth.*

—Manu Smriti – 2.239

Good things must be accepted, irrespective of where they come from. Poison is dangerous, but one can extract nectar even from poison. The Gods and demons churned the milky ocean with great difficulty and the first substance that arose was poison. Though frightened, they continued churning, and out came many things, good and bad. Finally, nectar arose. Thus, one may sift the good from the evil. One must find happiness even in the most distressful situation.

Generally, people do not pay much attention to the words of children and the young, for it is assumed that they do not have much knowledge and experience. But one must accept good words even though spoken by a child. A Sanskrit verse says that the gods call him wise, who is well learned and intelligent though he is young, but not the one who has grey hair. Similarly, good characters can be adopted even when they are found in enemies. For example, though the demons were evil, the good quality they had was patience. Gold, which is very precious, can similarly be extracted from dirt, though it blackens the hands, which can be washed later.

261. सद्भिरेव सहासीत सद्भिः कुर्वीत सङ्गतिम् ।
सद्भिर्विवादं मैत्रीं च नाऽसद्भिः किञ्चिदाचरेत् ॥

*One should associate with noble people. One should make friends with noble people. Arguments also should be had with noble people. But one should not have any kind of association with wicked people.*

**—Subhashita Ratnavali - 16.311**

The poet says that everything should be done in association with noble people, because we can always learn a lot from them. Thus, even quarrels and arguments can be had with noble people, rather than having friendship with wicked people. Another Sanskrit verse says that it is better to get kicked by a horse rather than ride a donkey! Here, the horse is compared to a noble man, as it is an animal of good qualities, while the donkey is compared to a wicked man.

262. प्रत्यहं प्रत्यवेक्षेत नरश्चरितमात्मनः ।
किं नु मे पशुभिस्तुल्यं किं नु सत्पुरुषैरिति ॥

*A man should analyse his character everyday thus: "Am I like an animal or am I like noble people?"*

— Subhashita Ratnavali - 14.541

It has been explained earlier that human beings remain distinct from all other animals in developing a good character. A man who builds good character is a real man, else he becomes equal to an animal. One should therefore analyse himself daily, as one looks at himself in the mirror. Just as one pays close attention to his hairstyle, dress etc when he looks in the mirror, he should also find faults within himself and correct them. Woodrow Wilson says, "Character is a by-product; it is produced in the great manufacture of daily duty."

263. अनुगन्तुं सतां वर्त्म कृत्स्नं यदि न शक्यते ।
स्वल्पमप्यनुगन्तव्यं मार्गस्थो नावसीदति ॥

*If it is not possible to follow the path of noble people fully, a little should be followed. A person then never falls from the right path.*

— Subhashita Ratnavali - 14.31

Everyone should become a noble man and serve the nation. This requires one to walk in the footsteps of great people. A child learns to speak by observing its mother and father speaking. Similarly, we should observe the actions of great people and follow them to some extent at least. It is not possible for every one of us to become a Mahatma Gandhi or Vivekananda, but if we adopt a few of their qualities, we can definitely rise to a higher plane than we otherwise would.

There is a story of two twin parrots. A hunter caught both and sold one of them to a wicked man, and the other to a sage. Both were taught to speak. The parrot in the wicked man's home would say: "Kill! Smash! Hit!" when guests came to his home, but the parrot at the sage's home would say,

"Welcome! Have a nice day! Thank you!" Thus, although both parrots were twins, they grew up in different environments and adopted contrasting qualities. Similarly, we too are originally pure, but if we associate with noble people, we would remain noble and if we associate with wicked people, we would become wicked.

www.ingramcontent.com/pod-product-compliance
Lightning Source LLC
Chambersburg PA
CBHW070331230426
**43663CB00011B/2280**